Papatango Theatre Compa
Finborough Theatre preser

The World Premiere of the w
Papatango New Writing Prize

COOLATULLY

by Fiona Doyle

FINBOROUGH | THEATRE

First performance at the Finborough Theatre, London:
Tuesday, 28 October 2014

COOLATULLY

by Fiona Doyle

Cast in order of appearance

Kilian	**Kerr Logan**
Eilish	**Yolanda Kettle**
Jimmy	**Eric Richard**
Paudie	**Charlie de Bromhead**

Director	**David Mercatali**
Designer	**Max Dorey**
Lighting Designer	**Christopher Nairne**
Sound Designer	**Max Pappenheim**
Dramaturg	**George Turvey**
Producer	**Chris Foxon**
Casting Director	**Emily Jones**
Assistant Director	**Joshua McTaggart**
Production Manager	**William Newman**
Stage Manager	**Roisin Symes**
Design Assistant	**Holly Hooper**
Production Assistant	**Justine Malone**

The action takes place in Ireland, in the present day.

The performance lasts approximately 90 minutes.

There will be no interval.

Our patrons are respectfully reminded that, in this intimate theatre, any noise such as rustling programmes, talking or the ringing of mobile phones may distract the actors and your fellow audience members.

We regret there is no admittance or re-admittance to the auditorium whilst the performance is in progress.

Cast and Creative Team

Charlie de Bromhead | Paudie
Productions at the Finborough Theatre include *The Pre-Raphaelites*, *Committed* and *The Immortal Memory*.

Trained at the London Academy of Music and Dramatic Art.

Theatre includes *How Many Miles to Babylon?* (Lyric Theatre, Belfast); *Charlie Peace: His Amazing Life and Astounding Legend* (Nottingham Playhouse); *Dandy Dick* (national tour); *Uncle Vanya* (Chichester Festival Theatre); *La Bohème* (Soho Theatre); *The Hostage* (Southwark Playhouse); *This Land* (West Yorkshire Playhouse); *Othello* (national tour); *Best Man Speech* (Flat Earth Theatre Company); *Pick 'N' Myths* (Lyric Theatre, Hammersmith) and *Cloud Cuckoo Land* (Riverside Studios).

Film includes *How to Lose Friends and Alienate People* and *Five Day Shelter*.

Television includes *Fair City*, *The Clinic* and *Aces Falling*.

Yolanda Kettle | Eilish
Trained at the London Academy of Music and Dramatic Art.

Theatre includes *Birdland* (Royal Court Theatre); *A Tale of Two Cities* (Royal & Derngate Theatre); *A Doll's House* (Young Vic Theatre and Duke of York's Theatre); *Pride and Prejudice* (Regent's Park Open Air Theatre); *Hello / Goodbye* (Hampstead Theatre); *The Seagull* (Arcola Theatre); *Saved* (Royal Court Gala); *The Mill on the Floss* and *Cabaret* (London Academy of Music and Dramatic Art) and *The Merchant of Venice* (National Youth Theatre).

Television includes *Father Brown*, *Mega Tsunami* and *Holby City*.

Kerr Logan | Kilian
Theatre includes *Teh Internet is Serious Business* (Royal Court Theatre) and *White Star of the North* (Lyric Theatre, Belfast).

Film includes *Good Vibrations*, *The Isis* and *Brothers*.

Television includes Mathos Seaworth in *Game of Thrones*, Conor in *London Irish*, *The Crimson Field*, *Six Degrees* and *Rites of Passage*.

Radio includes *Brief Lives*, *Eight Hundred and Thirty-Seven Point Nine*, *Maiden City Stories* and *Through the Wardrobe: The Belle Dress*.

Eric Richard | Jimmy
Theatre includes *Psych Warriors* (Crucible Theatre, Sheffield, and Royal Court Theatre); *Eejits* (Crucible Theatre, Sheffield, and Bush Theatre); *Chips with Everything* and *Antony and Cleopatra* (Birmingham Rep); *Chalk Circle* (Crucible Theatre, Sheffield); *One Flew Over the Cuckoo's Nest* (Royal Exchange Theatre, Manchester); *The Hostage* (Tricycle Theatre); *The Weir* (Haymarket Theatre, Basingstoke); *Lark Rise to Candleford* (national tour); *Diary of a Football Nobody* (Nottingham Playhouse) and *Loot* (national tour).

Eric was a founder member of Paines Plough.

Film includes Stephen Frears's *Prick Up Your Ears*, Mike Leigh's *Home Sweet Home* and Alan Clarke's *Made in Britain*.

Television includes Sergeant Bob Cryer in *The Bill*.

Fiona Doyle | Playwright
Coolatully is Fiona's debut full-length production.

Fiona completed the John Burgess Playwriting Course before undertaking a scholarship to study at the Universität der Künste, Berlin.

So Gay won the 2013 Play for the Nation's Youth and *Deluge* won the 2014 Eamon Keane Full-Length Play Award. Her short plays include *Rootbound* and *Rigor Mortis* (Arcola Theatre) and *Two Sisters* (Southwark Playhouse).

David Mercatali | Director
Productions at the Finborough Theatre include Anders Lustgarten's *Black Jesus*.

Theatre includes the world premiere of Timberlake Wertenbaker's *Our Ajax*, *Johnny Got His Gun* and *Feathers in the Snow* (Southwark Playhouse); *Sochi 2014* (Hope Theatre); *Someone to Blame* (King's Head Theatre); *Moonfleece* (Riverside Studios and national tour); *People's Day* (Pleasance London); *Runners the Return* (Underbelly at the Edinburgh Festival); *Weights* and *Paint Over* (Blue Elephant Theatre).

David won a 2013 Fringe First for his production of Philip Ridley's *Dark Vanilla Jungle* which transferred to the Soho Theatre in 2014, and was nominated for the Evening Standard Outstanding Newcomer Award for his production of *Tender Napalm* in 2011.

David is the Associate Director at Southwark Playhouse.

Max Dorey | Designer
Productions at the Finborough Theatre include *Black Jesus*.

Other theatre includes *Sleight & Hand* (Summerhall, Edinburgh Festival and BBC); *The Adventures of Count Ory* (Blackheath Halls); *I Can Hear You* and *This Is Not An Exit* (Royal Shakespeare Company at the Royal Court Theatre); *The School for Scandal* (Waterloo East Theatre); *The Duke in the Darkness* and *Marguerite*, both nominated for Off West End Awards for Best Set Design (Tabard Theatre); *Oedipus* (Blue Elephant Theatre); *Disco Pigs* (Tristan Bates Theatre); *The Good Soul of Szechuan*

(Bristol Old Vic Studio); *Macbeth* (Redgrave Theatre, Bristol); *Phaedra's Love* and *Bad House* (National Student Drama Festival); *Black Comedy* and *Playhouse Creatures* (Stage@Leeds).

Max has also made puppets for Travelling Light's *Peter Pan* (Bristol Old Vic); *Cinderella* (St James Theatre); *Pinocchio* (Tobacco Factory); *20,000 Leagues Under the Sea* (Birmingham Young Rep Company); *Phaedra's Love* and *The View From Down Here* – which he also wrote and directed (Ravenrock Theatre Company at the Carriageworks Theatre, Leeds).

Max trained in Theatre Design at Bristol Old Vic Theatre School, following a BA in English Literature and Theatre Studies at the University of Leeds.

In 2013, he was a finalist in the Linbury Prize for Stage Design, during which he worked with the National Theatre of Scotland. Max was Design Assistant at the Royal Shakespeare Company from 2013 to 2014.

Christopher Nairne | Lighting Designer
Productions at the Finborough Theatre include *The Captive*, *Generous* and *Oohrah!*

Theatre includes *Johnny Got His Gun* and *Our Ajax* (Southwark Playhouse); *Sense and Sensibility* (Watermill Theatre, Newbury); *Awkward Conversations with Animals I've F*cked* (Underbelly at the Edinburgh Festival); *The Me Plays* and *Mugs Arrows* (Old Red Lion Theatre); *Desdemona: A Play About a Handkerchief* and *The School for Scandal* (Park Theatre); *Dog Days* (Theatre503); *Dracula* (Theatre Royal, Bath); *The Ghost Hunter* (Old Red Lion Theatre and national tour); *Recording Hedda* (New Diorama Theatre); *Fiesta: The Sun Also Rises* and *Celebrity Night at Café Red* (Trafalgar Studios); *Boy in a Dress* (national tour). He was also Re-lighter for Complicite's 2013 UK tour of *Lionboy*.

Opera includes *Vivienne* (Royal Opera House); *La Calisto* (Hampstead Garden Opera); *In the Penal Colony* (Arts Theatre); *Belshazzar* (Trinity Laban Conservatoire); *The Adventures of Count Ory* (Blackheath Halls); *The Crocodile* (Riverside Studios) and the 2011 Olivier Award-winning *La Bohème* (OperaUpClose).

Max Pappenheim | Sound Designer
Productions at the Finborough Theatre include *This was a Man*, *Martine*, *Variation on a Theme*, *Black Jesus*, *Somersaults*, *The Soft of Her Palm* and *The Fear of Breathing*.

Theatre includes *Johnny Got His Gun*, *Three Sisters*, *Fiji Land* and *Our Ajax* (Southwark Playhouse); *Mrs Lowry and Son* (Trafalgar Studios); *CommonWealth* (Almeida Theatre); *Strangers on a Train* (English Theatre, Frankfurt); *The Distance* (Orange Tree Theatre); *Toast*, *The Man Who Shot Liberty Valance* and *The Archimedes Principle* (Park Theatre); *Das Ding* (New Diorama Theatre); *The Hotel Plays* (Defibrillator Theatre Company at The Langham Hotel); *Being Tommy Cooper* (national tour); *Irma Vep*, *Borderland* and *Kafka v Kafka* (Brockley Jack Theatre); *Freefall* (New Wimbledon Theatre Studio); *Four Corners One Heart* (Theatre503); *Awkward Conversations with Animals I've F*cked* (Underbelly at the Edinburgh Festival) and *Below the Belt* (Pleasance, Edinburgh Festival).

Associate Design includes *The Island* (Young Vic Theatre) and *Fleabag* (Soho Theatre).

Max was nominated in the Off West End Awards 2012 and 2014 for Best Sound Designer.

George Turvey | Dramaturg

George Turvey co-founded Papatango Theatre Company in 2007 and became the sole Artistic Director in January 2013.

He trained as an actor at the Academy of Live and Recorded Arts (ALRA) and has appeared on stage and screen throughout the UK and internationally, including playing the role of Batman in *Batman Live World Arena Tour*.

Direction includes *Leopoldville* (Papatango at the Tristan Bates Theatre) and *Angel* (Papatango at the Pleasance London and Tristan Bates Theatre).

As a dramaturg, he has overseen all of Papatango's productions.

Chris Foxon | Producer

Productions at the Finborough Theatre include *Unscorched* (Papatango New Writing Prize 2013); *I Didn't Always Live Here*; *Pack* and *Everyday Maps for Everyday Use* (Papatango New Writing Prize 2012) and *The Fear of Breathing*, which transferred in a new production to the Akasaka Red Theatre, Tokyo, in 2013.

Chris is the producer of Papatango Theatre Company.

Other productions include *Donkey Heart* (Old Red Lion Theatre); *The Keepers of Infinite Space* (Park Theatre); *Happy New* (Trafalgar Studios); *Tejas Verdes* (Edinburgh Festival) and *The Madness of George III* (Oxford Playhouse).

Productions as Assistant Producer include *Mudlarks* (HighTide Festival Theatre, Theatre503 and Bush Theatre) and *On the Threshing Floor* (Hampstead Theatre).

Chris was a Script Assessor and Assistant Project Manager for the T.S. Eliot Commissions at the Old Vic Theatre in 2013 and 2014.

Emily Jones | Casting Director

Productions at the Finborough Theatre include *The Hard Man* and *Unscorched* (Papatango New Writing Prize 2013).

Theatre includes *Donkey Heart* (Old Red Lion Theatre); *World Enough and Time, Fluff Shorts: No More Page 3* and *The Keepers of Infinite Space* (Park Theatre); *As You Like It* and *Richard III* (Changeling Theatre).

As assistant to Ginny Schiller, theatre includes *The Merchant of Venice* (Almeida Theatre); *The Hypochondriac* (Theatre Royal, Bath); *Bad Jews* (Ustinov Studio, Bath); *1984* (Headlong and West End); *Regeneration* (Royal & Derngate Theatre, Northampton); *Twelfth Night* (Everyman Theatre, Liverpool); *Relative Values* (Theatre Royal, Bath, and West End); *Fatal Attraction* (Theatre Royal, Haymarket); *Intimate Apparel* (Theatre Royal, Bath, and Park Theatre); *The Vibrator Play* (St James Theatre); *A Day in the Death of Joe Egg* (Rose Theatre, Kingston); *Pride and Prejudice* (Open Air Theatre, Regent's Park).

Film includes *Limbo* (JenX Films) and *Ibiza Undead* (Temple Heart Films).

Joshua McTaggart | Assistant Director
Joshua is the Resident Assistant Director at the Finborough Theatre, supported by the Richard Carne Trust, where he has assisted on *The Flouers O'Edinburgh* and a staged reading of *Little Red Hen*.

Trained with Diane Paulus and Shira Milikowsky at Harvard University and the American Repertory Theatre.

Theatre includes *the papier heart* (VAULT Festival 2013) and *pool (no water)*; *Sweeney Todd*; *The Tempest* (Harvard University).

Joshua was the Assistant Director for the Boston premieres of *She Kills Monsters* (Boston Centre for the Arts) and *The Lily's Revenge* (American Repertory Theatre).

William Newman | Production Manager
William Newman and the IOGIG team's clients include the Royal Opera House, Covent Garden, Glyndebourne, Northern Ballet, Qdos Entertainment and numerous West End shows.

Theatre includes includes *The Fizz* (W11 Opera); *Land of Our Fathers* (Theatre503); *Grimeborn* (Arcola Theatre); *Othello* (Guildford Shakespeare Company); *Nanny McPhee* (Sadler's Wells); *Microcosm* (Soho Theatre); *The China to Hackney Festival* (Hackney Empire).

Roisin Symes | Stage Manager
Productions at the Finborough Theatre include *Unscorched*, *Pack* and *Rigor Mortis* (all for Papatango).

Trained at the London Academy of Music and Dramatic Art.

Theatre includes *Eye of a Needle* and *Superior Donuts* (Southwark Playhouse); *Donkey Heart* (Old Red Lion Theatre); *The Matchgirls* (Wilton's Music Hall); *The Magpies*, *The Wolves* (Tristan Bates Theatre); *Orlando* (Battersea Arts Centre); *Many Moons* (Theatre503).

Holly Hooper | Design Assistant
Theatre includes *Bottleneck* (Hightide Festival Theatre); *My City* (Almeida Theatre); *Godchild* (Hampstead Theatre); *Macbeth* (Queensland Theatre Company).

Holly was also assistant designer for the Rifle Hall space at Hightide Festival Theatre. She is Production Manager and Design Coordinator for Kuleshov.

Justine Malone | Production Assistant
Theatre includes writing and performing *Asking for It* (Platform Theatre), devised with the Almeida Theatre. She recently won a place on Soho Theatre's Comedy Lab. Justine is a freelance script reader and editor, and writes for the online publications *One Stop Arts* and *Voice*.

She read English Literature at the University of Leeds and continued her studies at Birkbeck College. She was awarded the Birkbeck 2014 Shakespeare Prize for performance research, conducted at Shakespeare's Globe.

Production Acknowledgements

Papatango New Writing Prize 2014 Judging Panel | **Sam Donovan, Chris Foxon, Neil McPherson, Matt Roberts** and **George Turvey**

Papatango New Writing Prize 2014 Reading Team | **David Barnes, Joanna Bobin, Jonny Kelly** and **Justine Malone**

Press Representative | **Sue Hyman Associates Ltd** www.suehyman.com

Graphic Design | **Rebecca Maltby**

Production Photography | **Richard Davenport**

Workshop Venue | **Old School Room (Applecart Live)**

Rehearsal Venue | **Old Vic New Voices**

Special thanks to Arts Council England, the Backstage Trust, James Bobin, the Boris Karloff Charitable Foundation, the Foyle Foundation, the Garfield Weston Foundation, IdeasTap, Hannah Jenner, Old Vic New Voices, the Royal Victoria Hall Foundation, Kathryn Thompson and Ana Trayanova.

Coolatully was originally developed by Papatango with the following cast: Charlie de Bromhead, Stephen Myott-Meadows, Eric Richard and Fiona Ryan.

Papatango Theatre Company was founded in 2007 to find the best and brightest new writing in the UK with an absolute commitment to bringing this work to the stage.

Papatango have produced or developed new plays in venues including Bristol Old Vic, the Tristan Bates Theatre, the Old Red Lion Theatre, the Finborough Theatre and the Pleasance London, and our discoveries have been produced in many countries worldwide.

The Papatango New Writing Prize was launched in 2009, guaranteeing its winner a full four week production and publication by Nick Hern Books. The Papatango New Writing Prize is unique in UK theatre – no other new writing competition for full-length plays in the UK absolutely guarantees a full production and publication.

This reflects the company's mission to champion the best new talent and launch brilliant new theatre-makers with the greatest possible impact.

Previous winners of the Prize include Dominic Mitchell, who won a BAFTA this year for his BBC series *In The Flesh*, having been discovered and championed by Papatango who produced *Potentials*, his début show.

Other Prize-winners include Dawn King's *Foxfinder*, which was one of *The Independent's* Top Five Plays of the Year, won Dawn the OffWestEnd Award for Most Promising Playwright and the inaugural National Theatre Foundation Playwright Award and won the Critics' Circle Most Promising Newcomer Award for director Blanche McIntyre. *Foxfinder* has since been produced in Greece, Sweden, Germany, the USA, Australia and Iceland. Dawn and Blanche subsequently collaborated on the critically acclaimed national tour of *Ciphers* with Out of Joint.

2012 Prize-winner *Pack* by Louise Monaghan was described by Michael Billington in *The Guardian* as 'knock[ing] spots off much of the new writing I have seen'. Louise has since produced work with Octagon Theatre Bolton and Radio 4. Tom Morton-Smith, writer of our runner-up play *Everyday Maps for Everyday Use* in the same year, will have his play *Oppenheimer* produced by the Royal Shakespeare Company in 2015.

2013 Prize-winner Luke Owen's *Unscorched* will transfer to the Milano Playwriting Festival, Italy in 2015.

In 2014 Papatango established the position of Resident Playwright, funded by a BBC Theatre Fellowship and the Fenton Arts Trust. Our inaugural Resident Playwright, May Sumbwanyambe, went on to be commissioned by both National Theatre Scotland and Radio Four. In 2015 Samantha Potter will join us as our second Resident Playwright.

Papatango support not only brilliant new writers but develop the best creative talent in all disciplines. Our Assistant Director in 2011, Cathal Cleary, went on to win the JMK Award for Young Directors the following year, and our former Associate Director Bruce Guthrie has since directed in the West End and internationally.

Artistic Director | George Turvey
Producer | Chris Foxon
Artistic Associates | Sam Donovan, Matt Roberts
Resident Playwrights | Samantha Potter, May Sumbwanyambe

Board
David Bond
Sam Donovan
Zoe Lafferty
Nicholas Rogers

Patrons
Howard Davies CBE
Jeremy Gold
David Suchet OBE
Zoe Wanamaker CBE
Andrew Welch

Artistic Advisers
Colin Barr
Matt Charman
Tamara Harvey
Catherine Johnson
Dominic Mitchell
Con O'Neill
Tanya Tillett

2015 Papatango New Writing Prize
The Papatango New Writing Prize will return in autumn 2015 and will be
published by Nick Hern Books. Submissions will open in November 2014.
For details on how to enter, please go to www.papatango.co.uk/literary-
guidelines/.

Online
For up-to-date news and opportunities please visit:
www.facebook.com/pages/PapaTango-Theatre-Company/257825071298
www.twitter.com/PapaTangoTC
www.papatango.co.uk

Papatango Theatre Company Ltd is a registered charity and a company
limited by guarantee. Registered in England and Wales no. 07365398.
Registered Charity no. 1152789.

FINBOROUGH | THEATRE

VIBRANT **NEW WRITING** | UNIQUE **REDISCOVERIES**

'A disproportionately valuable component of the London theatre ecology. Its programme combines new writing and revivals, in selections intelligent and audacious.' *Financial Times*

'The tiny but mighty Finborough...one of the best batting averages of any London company.' Ben Brantley, *The New York Times*

'The Finborough Theatre, under the artistic direction of Neil McPherson, has been earning a place on the must-visit list with its eclectic, smartly curated slate of new works and neglected masterpieces.' *Vogue*

Founded in 1980, the multi-award-winning Finborough Theatre presents plays and music theatre, concentrated exclusively on vibrant new writing and unique rediscoveries from the 19th and 20th centuries. Our programme is unique – never presenting work that has been seen anywhere in London during the last 25 years. Behind the scenes, we continue to discover and develop a new generation of theatre makers – through our Literary team, and our programmes for both interns and Resident Assistant Directors.

Despite remaining completely unsubsidised, the Finborough Theatre has an unparalleled track record of attracting the finest talent who go on to become leading voices in British theatre. Under Artistic Director Neil McPherson, it has discovered some of the UK's most exciting new playwrights including Laura Wade, James Graham, Mike Bartlett, Sarah Grochala, Jack Thorne, Simon Vinnicombe, Alexandra Wood, Al Smith, Nicholas de Jongh, Dawn King, Chris Thompson and Anders Lustgarten; and directors including Blanche McIntyre.

Artists working at the theatre in the 1980s included Clive Barker, Rory Bremner, Nica Burns, Kathy Burke, Ken Campbell, Jane Horrocks and Claire Dowie. In the 1990s, the Finborough Theatre first became known for new writing including Naomi Wallace's first play *The War Boys*; Rachel Weisz in David Farr's *Neville Southall's Washbag*; four plays by Anthony Neilson including *Penetrator* and *The Censor*, both of which transferred to the Royal Court Theatre; and new plays by Richard Bean, Lucinda Coxon, David Eldridge, Tony Marchant and Mark Ravenhill. New writing development included the premieres of modern classics such as Mark Ravenhill's *Shopping and F***king*, Conor McPherson's *This Lime Tree Bower*, Naomi Wallace's *Slaughter City* and Martin McDonagh's *The Pillowman*.

Since 2000, new British plays have included Laura Wade's London debut *Young Emma*, commissioned for the Finborough Theatre; two one-woman shows by Miranda Hart; James Graham's *Albert's Boy* with Victor Spinetti; Sarah Grochala's *S27*; Peter Nichols' *Lingua Franca*, which transferred Off-Broadway; Dawn King's *Foxfinder*; and West End transfers for Joy Wilkinson's *Fair*; Nicholas de Jongh's *Plague Over England*; and Jack Thorne's *Fanny and Faggot*. The late Miriam Karlin made her last stage appearance in *Many Roads to Paradise* in 2008. We have also produced our annual festival of new writing – *Vibrant – A Festival of Finborough Playwrights* annually since 2009.

UK premieres of foreign plays have included plays by Brad Fraser, Lanford Wilson, Larry Kramer, Tennessee Williams, the English premiere of Robert McLellan's Scots language classic, *Jamie the Saxt*; and three West End transfers – Frank McGuinness' *Gates of Gold* with William Gaunt and John Bennett; and Craig Higginson's *Dream of the Dog* with Dame Janet Suzman.

Rediscoveries of neglected work – most commissioned by the Finborough Theatre – have included the first London revivals of Rolf Hochhuth's *Soldiers* and *The Representative*; both parts of Keith Dewhurst's *Lark Rise to Candleford*; Emlyn Williams' *Accolade*; Lennox Robinson's *Drama at Inish* with Celia Imrie and Paul O'Grady; John Van Druten's *London Wall* which transferred to St James' Theatre; and J. B. Priestley's *Cornelius* which transferred to a sell out Off Broadway run in New York City.

Music Theatre has included the new (premieres from Grant Olding, Charles Miller, Michael John LaChuisa, Adam Guettel, Andrew Lippa, Paul Scott Goodman, and Adam Gwon's *Ordinary Days* which transferred to the West End) and the old (the UK premiere of Rodgers and Hammerstein's *State Fair* which also transferred to the West End), and the acclaimed 'Celebrating British Music Theatre' series, reviving forgotten British musicals.

The Finborough Theatre won *The Stage* Fringe Theatre of the Year Award in 2011, *London Theatre Reviews'* Empty Space Peter Brook Award in 2010 and 2012, the Empty Space Peter Brook Award's Dan Crawford Pub Theatre Award in 2005 and 2008, the Empty Space Peter Brook Mark Marvin Award in 2004, and eight awards at the 2012 OffWestEnd Awards including Best Artistic Director and Best Director for the second year running. *Accolade* was named Best Fringe Show of 2011 by *Time Out*. It is the only unsubsidised theatre ever to be awarded the Channel 4 Playwrights Scheme (formerly the Pearson Playwriting Award) nine times. Three bursary holders (Laura Wade, James Graham and Anders Lustgarten) have also won the Catherine Johnson Award for Pearson Best Play.

www.finboroughtheatre.co.uk

FINBOROUGH | THEATRE

VIBRANT **NEW WRITING** | UNIQUE **REDISCOVERIES**

118 Finborough Road, London SW10 9ED
admin@finboroughtheatre.co.uk
www.finboroughtheatre.co.uk

Artistic Director | **Neil McPherson**
Resident Designer | Deputy Chief Executive | **Alex Marker**
General Managers | **Katy Hills** and **Daniel Fais**
Channel 4 Playwright-in-Residence | **Chris Thompson**
Playwrights-in-Residence | **Bekah Brunstetter, James Graham,
Dawn King, Anders Lustgarten** and **Shamser Sinha**
Playwrights on Attachment | **Steven Hevey, Louise Monaghan** and
Carmen Nasr
Associate Director (with the support of The Richard Carne Trust) |
Jennifer Bakst
Literary Manager | **Francis Grin**
Deputy Literary Manager | **Reen Polonsky**
Literary Assistants | **Miran Hadzic** and **Ben Lyon-Ross**
Technical Manager | **Matthew Sykes**
Associate Designer | **Philip Lindley**
Resident Producer | **Luke Holbrook**
Resident Casting Directors | **Lucy Casson, Hayley Kaimakliotis**
Resident Assistant Directors (with the support of The Richard Carne
Trust) | **Daniel Bailey** and **Joshua McTaggart**
Board of Trustees | **Stuart Worden** (Chair), **Davor Golub, Russell
Levinson, Dr Matthew Linfoot** and **Rebecca Maltby**.
And our many interns and volunteers.

The Finborough Theatre has the support of the Channel 4 Playwrights' Scheme,
sponsored by Channel 4 Television and supported by The Peggy Ramsay
Foundation.

Supported by
DLA Piper
the Richard Carne Trust Richardcarnetrust.Org

The Finborough Theatre is a member of the Independent Theatre Council, the
Society of Independent Theatres, Musical Theatre Network, The Friends of
Brompton Cemetery and The Earl's Court Society www.earlscourtsociety.org.uk

Mailing
Email admin@finboroughtheatre.co.uk or give your details to our Box Office staff to join our free email list. If you would like to be sent a free season leaflet every three months, just include your postal address and postcode.

Follow Us Online

 www.facebook.com/FinboroughTheatre

www.twitter.com/finborough

Feedback
We welcome your comments, complaints and suggestions. Write to Finborough Theatre, 118 Finborough Road, London SW10 9ED or email us at admin@finboroughtheatre.co.uk

Playscripts
Many of the Finborough Theatre's plays have been published and are on sale from our website.

Finborough Theatre T-shirts
Finborough Theatre T-shirts are now on sale from the Box Office £7.00.

Friends
The Finborough Theatre is a registered charity. We receive no public funding, and rely solely on the support of our audiences. Please do consider supporting us by becoming a member of our Friends of the Finborough Theatre scheme. There are various categories of Friends, each offering a wide range of benefits.

Richard Tauber Friends – Val Bond. James Brown. Tom Erhardt. Bill Hornby. Richard Jackson. Mike Lewendon. John Lawson. Harry MacAuslan. Mark and Susan Nichols. Sarah Thomas. Kathryn McDowall. Barry Serjent.

Lionel Monckton Friends – S. Harper. Philip G Hooker. Martin and Wendy Kramer. Deborah Milner. Maxine and Eric Reynolds.

William Terriss Friends – Stuart Ffoulkes. Leo and Janet Liebster. Peter Lobl. Paul and Lindsay Kennedy. Corinne Rooney. Jon and NoraLee Sedmak.

Smoking is not permitted in the auditorium and the use of cameras and recording equipment is strictly prohibited.

In accordance with the requirements of the Royal Borough of Kensington and Chelsea:

1. The public may leave at the end of the performance by all doors and such doors must at that time be kept open.
2. All gangways, corridors, staircases and external passageways intended for exit shall be left entirely free from obstruction whether permanent or temporary.

3. Persons shall not be permitted to stand or sit in any of the gangways intercepting the seating or to sit in any of the other gangways.

The Finborough Theatre is licensed by the Royal Borough of Kensington and Chelsea to The Steam Industry, a registered charity and a company limited by guarantee. Registered in England and Wales no. 3448268. Registered Charity no. 1071304. Registered Office: 118 Finborough Road, London SW10 9ED. The Steam Industry is under the overall Artistic Direction of Phil Willmott. www.philwillmott.co.uk

COOLATULLY

Fiona Doyle

Huge thanks to Papatango Theatre and David Mercatali for all their support during the development of this play.

And my mother; lifelong enthusiast for the fastest field sport on earth.

4

Characters

KILIAN DEMPSEY, *twenty-seven*
PADRAIG (PAUDIE) O'SULLIVAN, *twenty-eight*
EILISH O'CONNOR, *twenty-five*
JIMMY BARRETT, *seventies*

Note on Text

The play is set in the fictional village of Coolatully, somewhere on the southwest coast of Ireland.

Hurling is Ireland's national sport. It involves two teams of fifteen players each, a stick called a hurley and a small leather ball known as a sliotar. The game is said to be the fastest field sport on earth and has been traced as far back as the fifth century AD.

Cúchulainn is a mythological Irish hero. He once killed Culann's vicious hound in self-defence by hurling a sliotar into the beast's gaping mouth. Afterwards, he offered to guard Culann's fort himself until a replacement hound could be reared. From that day on, he was known as Cú Chulainn – 'the Hound of Culann'.

Sometimes Jimmy refers to Kilian as 'Kilian Óg' – 'Óg' is the Gaelic word for 'young'. It simply means, 'Young Kilian'.

A forward slash (/) marks the point where the immediately following dialogue or action interrupts.

This text went to press before the end of rehearsals and so may differ slightly from the play as performed.

Early December

A cold afternoon. KILIAN *is smoking by a grave.*

KILIAN. Cold out.

He smokes.

Like fuckin' Siberia.

He smokes.

You were never one for the cold. (*Pause.*) St Pat's won on Sunday. 2-12 to 1-14. What'shisname. O'Donovan. Centre half-forward. Few seconds to go 'cept then he scores this point out've nowhere. Coolatully nearly had it. They should've had it. Better side by far. Least they used be. (*Pause.*) Nights are drawin' in now. Gets dark early.

He smokes.

Tom Moriarty's off to New Zealand after Christmas. Construction's good out there. Fuckin' earthquakes every five seconds though. Imagine goin' to bed every night worrying 'bout the fuckin' building fallin' on your head. Nah, man. Fuck that. Not for me.

He zips up his jacket and pulls his hood over his head.

So Tom makes six. Six off the hurling team. Won't be any left to line out soon. Mark Drennan, Ron O'Callaghan, Michael Hayes, Liam Hayes, Dominic Joyce and now Tom. Disaster like. (*Beat.*) Don't mind so much 'bout Ron though. He's a prick. (*Pause.*) Good crowd in after. Even though we lost. Mam was pleased. But it's quiet the rest've the week. Don't open till the evening now. No one to serve. Jesus' sake, it's fuckin' freezin'!

Silence.

Time ticks by, hah?

He stubs out end of the fag and lights another. EILISH enters.

EILISH. Kilian.

KILIAN. Eilish.

She joins him at the grave.

EILISH. Cold today.

KILIAN. Fuckin' Siberian.

Pause.

EILISH. Used think it was hot there.

KILIAN. Hah?

EILISH. Siberia. When I was small. So I never understood what people meant when they said the weather was Siberian. 'Cause I always thought Siberia was like, this really hot place.

KILIAN. Their lakes freeze over.

Pause.

EILISH. Thought you'd be here. (*Pause.*) Did you cross the street?

KILIAN. Wha?

EILISH. When you saw me. Earlier on. Did you cross the street?

KILIAN. Course not.

EILISH. Liar. (*Pause.*) Can I've a drag?

KILIAN. You're a nurse.

She just looks at him.

Bad fer ya.

She raises one eyebrow. He gives her the cigarette. She takes a drag and hands it back. Silence.

EILISH. I've an interview up in Dublin next week. Hospital in Sydney. They'll help with all the visa stuff. I should just do it. Stupid not to. You can drive to Bondi Beach from there.

KILIAN *smokes*.

KILIAN. D'you hear 'bout Tom Moriarty?

EILISH. Yeah. New Zealand. After Christmas. (*Beat*.) I hate Christmas.

KILIAN. That's half the team now.

EILISH. Well there's nothin' here for 'em.

Pause.

KILIAN. Never gonna happen.

EILISH. Should get out while you can.

KILIAN. Can't leave the mam on her own with the pub.

EILISH. It's your life.

KILIAN. Barely breaking / even.

EILISH. It's your life.

Silence.

KILIAN. The heat'll be good, hah? Fer a change. Mind the earthquakes though. And the fires. I hear the fires out there are ferocious.

He smokes.

Silence.

She exits.

He stubs out his cigarette.

Jesus. Eight months. (*Pause*.) Fuckin' hell, Seamus. (*Places his hand on the grave*.)

Later that day. JIMMY*'s front room in a remote cottage, about two miles outside Coolatully.* JIMMY *is asleep in his chair by the fire. A hurley stick leans up against a wall near the fireplace. A radio is on low in the background. Someone knocks on the door.* JIMMY *doesn't stir. Someone knocks again.* JIMMY *opens one eye and grunts.*

KILIAN. Jimmy? You in?

    JIMMY *curses, gets to his feet.*

JIMMY. D'you not have yer key?

KILIAN. I do, yeah.

JIMMY. Then feckin' use it!

    Key turns and KILIAN *enters with a shopping bag.*

KILIAN. Ah, no need to get up, Jim, I'm in now.

    He starts unpacking the few groceries.

JIMMY. What good'll you be to me if I have a fall some day, hah?

KILIAN. Shit. Forgot / the biscuits.

JIMMY. Stretched out on that cold hard floor with blood all down my face from the gaping crack in the back've my skull, and what'll you be doin'? Waitin' outside. Knockin' politely. Wondering if you can come in.

KILIAN. Your usual sparkly self I see. S'fuckin' cold out there today.

JIMMY. What d'you want?

KILIAN. Well now that you mention it I wouldn't mind a cup've tea.

JIMMY. You look like shit.

KILIAN (*ignoring this*). Taken your medicine today?

JIMMY. Aye, fer all the good it's doin'. An' see this here – (*Shows him his right hand. The fingers are bent slightly.*) They won't go back. That's a new thing that is. Just like the father.

KILIAN. Ya look like Captain Hook's cousin.

JIMMY. I'll Captain Hook you in a minute.

KILIAN (*exits to kitchen*). D'you've a basin?

JIMMY. What for?

KILIAN (*calling*). Lukewarm water. Might soften the joints a bit.

JIMMY. Under the sink. Not the green one though, there's a hole in that. Old age. It's a feckin' curse!

KILIAN. Had fun gettin' there though, didn't ya? Jimmy Barrett, yer kitchen's a fuckin' disgrace!

JIMMY. 'Tis grand! Leave it now an' don't go upsettin' things!

KILIAN. I wanted a cup've tea!

JIMMY. Well go on an' make one then!

KILIAN (*entering with a towel and basin, places basin on a side table*). I would if I could find a cup.

JIMMY (*putting his hand into the water*). Can put my hands on anything I need in there.

KILIAN. Sherlock Holmes couldn't find a fuckin' cup in there.

JIMMY. Anything! Including your neck. An' I've a system, so leave it alone.

KILIAN. What system's that now? The leave-yer-crap-all-over-the-place system?

JIMMY. Cheeky pup.

KILIAN. An' where's yer stick?

JIMMY. In the bedroom.

KILIAN. Why's it out there?

JIMMY. 'Cause I don't need it in here.

KILIAN. Yes you do. You've had a hip replacement, for Christ's sake.

JIMMY. Are you the boss've me now, are ya?

KILIAN. Yer an awful stubborn old git sometimes, d'you know / that?

JIMMY. An' did you know, that if you corner a badger he'll grip on to an arm or a leg an' he won't let go fer love nor money? An' the only way to free yerself is to look fer a twig or a bit've a branch an' snap it in two. 'Cause then the badger thinks he's broken a bone see, an' off he goes.

KILIAN (*beat*). What?!

JIMMY. Don't say I never taught ya nothin'. (*Closes his eyes and enjoys the sensation of the water for a few moments.*) So. We were robbed on Sunday. Shame. They're still missing you out on that pitch, boy. It's a bloody waste.

KILIAN. D'you've any biscuits? (*Goes out to kitchen again.*)

JIMMY. Fastest field sport on earth y'know. The mighty Cúchulainn himself used play it. Sure didn't he kill the vicious hound with the stick and sliotar.

KILIAN (*re-enters eating a biscuit*). So the story goes.

JIMMY. Bit've truth in all stories, boy.

KILIAN. Did ya know these are stale?

JIMMY. A man lived here once. Distant relative they used say. You'd see him early in the morning high up on the clifftops practising his swing. Half-naked he'd be. Big giant of a man see. The clothes wouldn't fit him right. One time, we saw him there in the dead of winter. The cliffs all white with snow an' he barefoot with the stick. Steam comin' off him. Striking from the hand again and again. An' every time he struck he'd let out this almighty roar, an' the land would shake beneath him, an' the birds would go screeching and scattering over the waves.

KILIAN (*beat*). Right. (*Opens a newspaper.*)

JIMMY. 'Do not, henceforth, use the plays which men call horlings, with great sticks and a ball upon the ground, from which many evils and maims have arisen.' Who was that?

KILIAN. Ah Jesus, Jimmy, I dunno.

JIMMY. Think, boy, think!

KILIAN (*reluctantly*). Fuckin'… Edward the fourth?

JIMMY. Third! Tried to ban it so he did. The fool. Sure isn't there graves up there in Donegal from the fifteenth century with the stick and sliotar carved into rock like the Holy / Cross itself.

KILIAN. D'you hear Tom Moriarty's off to New Zealand by the way?

JIMMY. What?

KILIAN. After Christmas.

JIMMY. Sure that's half the flippin' team gone then! Tom's a fine player.

KILIAN. Ah he's alright. Bit overrated if you ask me.

JIMMY. *You* are a fine player an' you should be playing still, fit an' young like you are. But you won't be fit an' young / for ever, boy!

KILIAN. Never thought he'd leave. Bit of a mammy's boy Tom is.

JIMMY. They used call you Cúchulainn. It's not right that you don't play / no more.

KILIAN. An' d'you hear about the post office?

JIMMY. What about the post office?

KILIAN. They're closing.

JIMMY. Ah fer… sure nearest one now'll be twenty mile off. Where'll I draw me pension?

KILIAN. I'll take you to the town if ya want.

JIMMY. On that yoke of a bike? You will not.

KILIAN. I'll *drive* ya.

JIMMY. Sure you don't have a car.

KILIAN. Can borrow the mam's. An' that's a good bike by the way.

JIMMY. Anyway, I wouldn't get into a car with you fer love nor money. Sure you had to do the test three times before you passed.

KILIAN. I'll put you in the fuckin' boot of the car in a minute so I will.

JIMMY. First the Garda Station. Now the post office. Might as well close down the whole feckin' village at this rate.

KILIAN. Ned was near retirement age anyway I s'pose.

JIMMY. Bullockcrap. Sure everyone knows he's never been right since what happened. They held a gun to his head, for Christ's sake.

KILIAN. A fake one.

JIMMY. Well Ned didn't know that, did he! State've us. They found a head up in Dublin.

KILIAN. Hah?

JIMMY. Oh yeah. Little boy came across it lodged between two rocks in a stream behind an estate in Ballyfermot. Wrapped in plastic. No body. God love the child. He thought it was a football.

KILIAN *grimaces and goes back to newspaper.* JIMMY *studies him for a moment.*

Any work on the horizon?

KILIAN. What d'you think.

JIMMY. Dole's no life for a man.

KILIAN. You know the story.

JIMMY. Not what they drew blood for back / in 1916.

KILIAN. Ah Jesus, Jimmy, don't start with the / 1916 stuff again.

JIMMY. Not what James Connolly was hoping for when they tied him to that chair. Or when they shot him through the heart. Ow!

KILIAN. Sorry.

KILIAN*'s now drying* JIMMY*'s hand with a towel.*

JIMMY. But you need to go. Canada maybe. Or New Zealand. There's work in those places for fellas in the building trade.

KILIAN. I can't leave the mam on her own with the pub. How many times do I've to tell ya. Anyway, sure wouldn't I miss yer whinging. (*Takes basin back out to kitchen*.)

JIMMY (*to himself*). 'But today it is my father who keeps stumbling behind me, and will not go away.' (*Massages his hand*.) So when's yer good-fer-nothin' little eejit of a friend out then?

KILIAN (*calling*). He's another month to go yet. Goin' up to see him next week.

JIMMY. He'll be in for Christmas so.

KILIAN. He will.

We hear the sound of a small window being closed.

JIMMY. I don't suppose he's learned how to make himself useful in there? At a guess I'd say not.

KILIAN (*re-entering with a glass of water. Hands it to JIMMY who takes some tablets from his pocket and swallows two pills*). He did a woodwork class a while back. Made a doll's house. Seven rooms. Little bathroom with a toilet an' everything.

JIMMY. Yeah, 'cause there's great demand for them doll's houses round these parts. Queuing out the door for 'em. Padraig O'Sullivan's a little shit an' he'll be back in prison before you know it. Mark my / words.

KILIAN. I'll tell him you were askin' fer him then, will I?

Silence. JIMMY *stokes the fire*.

What're you havin' fer the dinner?

JIMMY. There's a few lamb chops in the freezer.

KILIAN. Will I take one out fer ya?

JIMMY. Did I *ask* you to take one out fer me?

KILIAN. Well do you *want* me to take... yer being fierce difficult today, d'you / know that?

JIMMY. If I want you to take one out fer me, then I'll ask you to take one out / fer me.

KILIAN. You should be taking it / easy.

JIMMY. You stop tellin' me what to do! I was a strong man once. Built roads once. Danced up a storm once. (*Pause*.) She'll need you for opening up soon. Get down on one knee there and pull up that floorboard.

KILIAN. Hah?

JIMMY (*pointing*). Just do it!

> KILIAN *goes down on his knees*.

No, not that one.

KILIAN. Which one then?

JIMMY. That one.

KILIAN. This one?

JIMMY. That's it. See the edge jutting out? Lift it up. That's right, there you go. Lift it.

> KILIAN *does and the board comes loose. He looks in*.

Take one out.

> KILIAN *reaches in and pulls out a biscuit tin*.

Well go on, open it.

> KILIAN *opens it and stares inside*.

It's not all for you. Just take a twenty. Fer yer trouble like. Nice little spot, hah? Thought you'd be pleased. Not under the bed any more.

KILIAN. I've told you, Jim, you can't keep so much cash about the place!

JIMMY. I'll keep doin' it the way I've always done it.

KILIAN. Should be in the bank.

JIMMY. Bastard banks. Ruined the country. Don't be lecturing me, Kilian Óg. Take a twenty an' feck off.

KILIAN (*putting tin back and replacing floorboard*). Dropping in on a friend is all. Don't need paying for that. An' what about a break-in?

JIMMY. There'll be no break-in.

KILIAN. What about the post office? An' Mrs Reilly's place was broken in to last month.

JIMMY. Ah sure wasn't that only her gombeen of a nephew off his head on the drugs. They say she gave him a right good hiding after. Anyway. D'you know what they'd get fer their trouble? (*Indicates hurley stick.*) A crack over the head with that. That's what.

KILIAN. Yeah, an' then you'd be up fer assault. (*Pause.*) Will I bring in a few briquettes before I go?

JIMMY *just points at the door.* KILIAN *shakes his head and goes to exit.*

That's a stupid place to keep yer money.

JIMMY. Regards to yer mother.

KILIAN (*stopping at door*). By the way, what happens if you get cornered by more than one?

JIMMY. Hah?

KILIAN. Badger.

JIMMY (*beat*). Sure yer a feckin' eejit if that happens. Deserve a broken bone then so you do.

KILIAN. Fair enough. Right, see you tomorrow.

JIMMY. If you've time.

KILIAN. Sure I've plenty of that these days. Left the basin on the sink.

KILIAN *exits.* JIMMY *looks after him, shaking his head, muttering something about 'a waste'. He turns up the radio. A programme dedicated to Irish showband music has started. They're playing Dickie Rock's 1966 hit 'Come Back to Stay'. JIMMY smiles and stokes the fire. Then he leans back in his chair, closes his eyes and hums along with the song.*

Mid-January

A Monday. The pub is empty. There's a back door upstage left.
There's a front door somewhere too but no one ever uses that.
Christmas has come and gone. KILIAN *is behind the bar*
reading a newspaper. There are still a few Christmas
decorations around the place. Footsteps approach from outside.
The back door opens and PAUDIE *enters.* KILIAN *comes out*
from behind the bar. Pause.

PAUDIE. Christ, boy. You look like shit.

KILIAN. Had a look in a mirror yourself lately?

   They embrace.

   Fuckin' hell, man, why didn't ya tell me? Thought it was
   next week?

PAUDIE. Sure I said I'd surprise ya.

KILIAN. I've not had a chance to put up the balloons or
   anything.

PAUDIE. Yeah right, be lucky to get a bag've crisps outta you.
   Speaking of which, I'm fuckin' starvin'.

KILIAN. Sit down there. (*Goes behind bar and throws him a*
   bag of crisps, then starts pulling a pint.)

PAUDIE. Ready salted. Don't get these inside unless you're
   very good.

KILIAN. Should've told me, man. Would've taken the night off.

PAUDIE (*eating*). Sure what's the difference? We'd be sat in
   here anyway. So. How's things?

KILIAN. Same old. You?

PAUDIE (*eating*). Like a pig in shit.

KILIAN. D'you tell Eilish?

PAUDIE. On her way, boy. On her way. Christ it's good to be
   back. How Mandela did it I'll never know.

KILIAN. As in Nelson?

PAUDIE. No, as in Jim Bob.

KILIAN. You were in for six months, ya feckin' eejit.

PAUDIE. I feel a great affinity with the man now is all I'll say.

KILIAN. They put him in solitary confinement. With a slop
bucket. An' he had to crush rocks!

PAUDIE. A feeling of kinship, boy. A feeling of kinship.

KILIAN *rolls his eyes.*

Jesus. Dead in here or what.

KILIAN. Middle've January. Monday night.

PAUDIE. Still though. Fuckin' ghost town.

KILIAN. Post-Christmas slump.

PAUDIE. Coolatully fuckin' slump is what it is.

KILIAN (*putting pint down*). There you go, Mandela, get that
down ya.

PAUDIE. *Sláinte.* (*Downs pint and lets out a huge belch.*)
Home sweet home.

KILIAN (*pulling another pint*). Where the buffalo roam.

PAUDIE. More like the cows really.

KILIAN. An' the sheep.

PAUDIE. An' Mrs Reilly.

KILIAN. She missed you.

PAUDIE. Like a hole in the head. (*Noticing decorations.*) Can't
be arsed to take them down?

KILIAN. Couldn't be arsed puttin' them up in the first place.

PAUDIE. Sure they'll do ya for next year. The guy two cells up
from me grew his own hash plant. They never copped a
thing. Christmas Eve right, he decorates it. Little baubles an'
everthing. In fer tax evasion. Three years. Called him the
Dice Man.

KILIAN (*giving* PAUDIE *his second pint*). Three years?

PAUDIE. Two suspended. Used be a blocklayer. Four small
kiddies an' all. Gave me three spliffs Christmas morning.
Sound guy.

KILIAN. Sorry I couldn't make it up on the day.

PAUDIE. Ah, ya had your mam to worry 'bout. (*Pause*.) Last week right, this new fella comes in. Next thing, he's taken off to have a hundred and thirty-five stitches put in his head.

KILIAN. Jesus.

PAUDIE . Killed his own baby.

KILIAN. Well then he fuckin' deserved it.

PAUDIE. Said it was an accident. Anyway. S'all done now. Onwards. (*Drinks*.)

KILIAN. Onwards.

PAUDIE. Seriously though, how's things? You really do look like shit.

KILIAN. Just... tired.

PAUDIE. Not havin' one yerself?

KILIAN. Nah. I'm working.

PAUDIE *looks deliberately around the empty pub.*

I'm still meant to be working.

PAUDIE. She's not even payin' ya!

KILIAN. 'Cause we're barely breakin' even!

PAUDIE. Ah have a drink, man, for the love of God.

KILIAN *gets himself a drink.*

Hey.

KILIAN. Wha?

PAUDIE. Knock knock.

KILIAN. No!

PAUDIE. Ah go on.

KILIAN. I did not miss this.

PAUDIE. Knock knock!

KILIAN. Who's fuckin' there.

PAUDIE. Hava.

KILIAN. Hava fuckin' who.

PAUDIE. Don't say 'Hava fuckin' who'. 'Cause that just spoils it. Say it the way yer meant to say it or don't say it at all.

KILIAN. I won't say it at all then.

PAUDIE. Fine.

KILIAN. Grand.

Pause.

PAUDIE. Ah go on.

KILIAN. Fuck's sake. Hava who?

PAUDIE. Hava Happy New Year! (*Beat.*) I just made that up.

KILIAN. S'fuckin' awful.

They toast and drink.

PAUDIE. Been down there lately?

KILIAN. Down there most days. (*Pause.*) Headstone next. Need at least a grand for it. Then there's the base, kerbs, corner posts, inscriptions. I'm tellin' ya, good money in death. She wants a Celtic cross with some bullshit on it 'bout the light of heaven. In Irish. All he could ever say in Irish was 'Can I go to the toilet please?'

PAUDIE (*like a child to a teacher*). *An bhfuil cead agam dul go dtí an leithreas más é do thoil é?* [Can I go to the toilet please?]

They laugh. Then silence.

We need to go.

KILIAN. Can't. Sure amn't I working.

PAUDIE. No, ya eejit, I mean we need to *go*. Get the fuck out've here.

KILIAN (*pointing upstairs*). State've her at the moment? Doesn't get out of bed at all some days.

PAUDIE. Listen, how long've you been on the dole?

KILIAN. Everyone's on the fuckin' dole.

PAUDIE. There's work out there for people like us. Canada. Australia. New Zealand. We're skilled labour.

KILIAN. You know why there's work in places like New Zealand? 'Cause of all the earthquakes. They're in the fuckin' earthquake / zone.

PAUDIE. Who gives a shit! Prefer to go out in an earthquake than… (*Points at* KILIAN.) Quantity surveyor – (*Points to himself.*) Electrician. We're on the S–O–L.

KILIAN looks at him blankly.

Skilled Occupation List? Australia? Means we get visas easier. Means they're practically begging us to go over. Everyone fuckin' loves the Irish out there. Think about it. The beaches. The weather. The fit half-naked women. No more queueing down the poxy dole office. With the peeling plaster and the stink of stale tobacco from yer man in front of you who couldn't be bothered to wash that morning. Or worse, queueing *outside* the poxy dole office. 'Cause the people with the jobs on the inside are finishing their sandwiches an' their nice cups of tea, leavin' you stood out there like a muppet in the rain. Rain that isn't even proper rain 'cause nothing here can be arsed any more. It's just drizzly-fuckin'-spittin'-at-you-half-arsed-can't-be-fuckin'-bothered rain 'cause it's goddamn Irish rain and we can't do it properly!

KILIAN. Ah c'mon now. If there's one thing we know how to do properly.

Silence.

We'd need money.

PAUDIE. We'll get it.

KILIAN. How?

PAUDIE. Where there's a will.

KILIAN. I'm on the dole. You're just out've prison.

PAUDIE. Don't do that.

KILIAN. Do what?

Footsteps approach and stop outside the door. EILISH *enters.*

PAUDIE. There she is! The most beautiful girl in the County!

EILISH. The only girl in the fuckin' County. How are ya, ya big criminal.

PAUDIE. I paid it back! Every penny!

EILISH. Yeah, with interest.

They embrace.

PAUDIE. Get the woman a drink, Kil.

KILIAN. I'd say she's had enough.

EILISH. Fuck off.

PAUDIE. My sentiments exactly.

KILIAN. Fine.

KILIAN *pours her a drink.* PAUDIE *and* EILISH *sit down.*

EILISH. You've cut your hair.

PAUDIE. Cost me a coffee an' four smokes. Not bad though, hah?

EILISH. Never seen it so short. (*Beat.*) You look a bit like an otter.

PAUDIE. Wha?!

EILISH. Did I say that out loud?

PAUDIE. Fuck you!

EILISH. I'm just not used to seeing your ears!

PAUDIE. What's wrong with my ears?!

KILIAN. I think he looks a bit like that meerkat fella.

EILISH. Comparethemarket dot com?

KILIAN. Yeah! That's it. What'shisname, Sergei from Comparethemarket.

PAUDIE. Fuckin' great homecomin' this is!

EILISH (*ruffling his hair*). So, Sergei, were they all sad to see you leave.

PAUDIE. Gutted. I'd a few've of them in tears. Guards all chipped in an' threw me a goin'-away party. Yeah, they went to town like. Big bouncy castle, U2 tribute band, all-you-can-eat buffet with ham an' pineapple pizza and these little handmade profiteroles. There was even banoffee pie. Yeah, it was like Butlins really only you couldn't leave.

EILISH. D'you get yer Christmas pressie? Or did the guards take it off ya fer being bold.

PAUDIE. I did. I got me Christmas pressie. (*To* KILIAN.) Eilish sent me a Christmas pressie.

KILIAN. I sent you a fuckin' Christmas pressie.

PAUDIE. Hers was nicer. Thought I might get out early. But they liked me too much. Bastards.

EILISH. Well next time don't take stuff that isn't yours.

PAUDIE. I'll miss that car.

KILIAN. You can borrow my bike.

PAUDIE. Great.

EILISH. D'you hear someone broke into the church last night by the way?

PAUDIE (*putting his hands in the air*). I only got out this morning!

EILISH. Doors need replacing. Father Ryan's fuming.

KILIAN. He's always fuming 'bout somethin'.

EILISH. Used a pickaxe. An' a sledgehammer.

PAUDIE. Fuckin' eejits. Why didn't they just go through the window?

KILIAN (*handing* EILISH *her drink*). Ah I couldn't. I'd feel bad about Mikey Donovan's stained glass.

PAUDIE. Was it Mikey Donovan did that stained glass?

KILIAN. D'you not remember?

EILISH. That was his first commission.

PAUDIE. Was it? Fuck. That's impressive. Real skill that. Art like. Yeah, I see why they went fer the door now. (*To* EILISH.) So. How are ya? Any *scéal* [news]?

EILISH. Oh y'know, off to Australia. (*Glances at* KILIAN.)

PAUDIE. Serious?

EILISH. Got a job in a teaching hospital near Sydney. Ten-minute drive to Bondi Beach.

PAUDIE. D'you hear that, Kil? Ten-minute drive to Bondi Beach. When you off?

EILISH. Few months. Found out today. There's even an agency to sort out the paperwork.

PAUDIE. Ten-minute drive to fuckin' Bondi Beach.

EILISH. You earn twice as much out there.

PAUDIE. I know! I keep tellin' him! 'Cept he's afraid of the fuckin' earthquakes!

KILIAN. Fuck off.

EILISH. What about the record though?

PAUDIE. Twelve months or more might be a problem but I was out in six. An' I ain't hangin' round just to rot in Coolatully. (*Looks at* EILISH.) We'll miss ya.

EILISH *drinks*.

EILISH. Christ. Dead in here.

KILIAN. It's a Monday night!

PAUDIE. First night of freedom, fer fuck's sake. Where is everyone?

EILISH. Gone.

KILIAN. Mark Drennan went last August.

EILISH. An' Ron O'Callaghan left just after him.

PAUDIE. Well. Ron's no loss, he's a prick.

KILIAN. Michael Hayes, Liam Hayes an' Dominic Joyce left together last...?

EILISH. October.

PAUDIE. All of 'em?

EILISH. Even Tom Moriarty's gone.

PAUDIE. Tom Moriarty?

EILISH. He's in New Zealand now.

PAUDIE. D'you hear that, Kil? Even fuckin' Tom Moriarty's gone. The biggest mammy's boy in all've Ireland an' even he's gone.

EILISH. Ah he's not a mammy's boy.

PAUDIE/KILIAN. He fuckin' is.

PAUDIE. Hey, d'you remember the bee?

KILIAN *laughs*.

EILISH. What bee?

PAUDIE. Years back right? Third class an' Tom's chasin' Seamus round the yard. What'd he done again?

KILIAN. Tried to pull his pants down.

PAUDIE. That's the one. Seamy tried to pull Tom's pants down in front of us all. So Tom's chasin' him right? The two of 'em flyin' down the yard full-throttle, Tom screamin' his head off, mouth wide open – (*Imitating Tom.*) 'I'll tell me mam on you, I'll tell me mam!' So they're legging it down the yard, then next thing, Tom stops dead, hands up to his throat like this. (*Demonstrates.*) Face goin' blue, eyes bulgin' – (*Makes choking sounds.*)

EILISH. Jesus. What happened?

KILIAN. He'd swallowed a bee.

PAUDIE*'s killing himself laughing*.

EILISH. Swallowed a bee?

KILIAN. Yeah.

EILISH. That's not funny.

PAUDIE (*barely able to talk*). It was. It was fuckin' hilarious!

KILIAN. They took him off after to get a shot or somethin.' Bee probably died from lack of oxygen anyway.

PAUDIE. An' then the best bit right, Seamy comes back over 'cause he could see that Tom was choking, so he comes back over to see if he's alright, an' Tom just… kicks him in the balls! Still chokin' an' clawin' at his neck like, but his legs were free, so he just kicks him right in the bollox! Seamy was fucked for days.

Crying with laughter. EILISH *starts laughing.* KILIAN *starts laughing. The laughter gradually dies down. Silence.*

Let's get pissed.

EILISH. Yeah. Something new fer a change.

KILIAN *gets some more drinks.* PAUDIE *goes behind the bar where the CD player is.*

PAUDIE. D'you know what we need? We need music. That's what we need.

KILIAN. No licence any more.

PAUDIE. What?

KILIAN. Cuts down on costs.

PAUDIE. Fer fuck's sake!

KILIAN. We can't put any music on.

PAUDIE. Are you fuckin' serious?

KILIAN. Yes! What am I meant to do? We've no licence / any more!

PAUDIE. Ah! Hang on a sec! Where's yer licence fer talkin'?

KILIAN. Paudie, stop being / a fuckin' eejit.

PAUDIE. Shut up till I see yer licence fer talkin'.

EILISH. An' walkin'. Have you a licence fer that?

PAUDIE. An' goin' to the toilet. See them toilets over there? Well you can't use them till I see yer licence.

EILISH. Go on, Kil. He might start singing otherwise.

PAUDIE. I will! I'll start singing! I swear to God I will!

KILIAN. Jesus! Put something on then but keep it low.

PAUDIE searches for something to play.

EILISH. Any Pogues there?

KILIAN. Keep it low.

EILISH. He loved The Pogues.

PAUDIE (*to* EILISH). Will we have a little dance?

EILISH. Last time I had a little dance I twisted my ankle, or rather *you* twisted it for me with yer big hobbit feet.

PAUDIE. I'll have you know I've a nice pair of feet I do.

We hear 'Dirty Old Town' by The Pogues.

KILIAN. That's too loud.

PAUDIE. Christ. Who are you, my mother?

KILIAN places drinks on the bar. He turns the music down. PAUDIE looks at him, then gives him the finger and turns it back up.

KILIAN. Paudie, I'll fuckin' kill / ya!

EILISH. Oh fer Christ's sake. (*Turns the volume halfway.*) There. Okay?

KILIAN. Fuckin' eejit.

PAUDIE. You're a fuckin' eejit.

EILISH. Ye're both fuckin' eejits!

They laugh, drink, chat and mess around as the song plays on.

EILISH *is asleep in bed.* KILIAN *is sitting beside her smoking.*
She wakes.

EILISH. Can't sleep?

> KILIAN *shakes his head and smokes.*

> What time is it?

KILIAN (*shrugging shoulders*). Still dark outside.

EILISH (*sits up*). Pass the water will you?

> *He passes her a glass of water, she drinks.*

> Patient says 'Doctor? I can't get to sleep at night at all. What
> should I do?' Doctor says 'Lie on the edge of the bed an'
> you'll soon drop off.'

> KILIAN *rolls his eyes.*

> S'one of Paudie's.

KILIAN. It's shit.

> *Silence.*

EILISH. What're you thinking?

KILIAN. I'm thinking… I'm thinking about the sandwiches.

EILISH. What?

KILIAN. I'm thinking about the sandwiches for the anniversary.

EILISH. Kilian, it's a good three months / off yet.

KILIAN. I'm thinking ham an' cheese, an' then just plain
cheese for the veggies.

> *Pause.*

EILISH. I need to sleep.

> *She lies back down.*

KILIAN. This is wrong.

EILISH. Right. Well why are you sitting in my bed then? (*Grabs
the cigarette from his mouth.*) An' you know I don't like that.
The ash gets in the sheets. (*Stubs it out.*) He's not here.

KILIAN. Don't.

EILISH. He's not here, Kilian.

KILIAN. Stop fuckin' sayin' it like that.

EILISH. Like what?

KILIAN. Like you're glad.

> *She immediately slaps him hard across the face. Silence.*
> KILIAN *rubs his face.*

That was a shit thing to say. I'm sorry.

EILISH (*her voice is raised now*). We were sixteen years old,
for Christ's sake. S'all a lifetime ago now. Ten / years
almost.

KILIAN. He was crazy about you. Right till the end, he was
always crazy about you.

EILISH. This isn't about me!

> *He looks at her. He looks away. He smokes.*

Look at you. Slumping. Slumped down like an old man.

> *He stands up and continues smoking by the window, his back
> to her.*

You made the County Team once. Now your fingers are all
yellow.

> *Someone knocks on the bedroom door.*

Shit.

> *She grabs a dressing gown and leaves the room. We hear
> muffled voices in the hallway. She re-enters.*

Jesus Christ. I hate this place. D'you know what, just…
fuck off. Yeah? Go on. Leave! *You* can't sleep. Which
means *I* can't sleep. And I *need* to sleep 'cause I've got an
early start tomorrow so fuck off, Kilian, an' go an' not sleep
somewhere else.

KILIAN *starts dressing.*

That shirt's on inside out.

He stops, looks at her, then sits on bed and puts his head in his hands.

You can't live your life for someone else.

KILIAN. She's my mam.

EILISH. She has to learn how to cope. I won't wait for ever y'know. This isn't some... fucking Disney film. I want things to start again.

Silence.

KILIAN. What about the earthquakes?

EILISH. Listen, if a big crack opened up in the earth's surface right now, right this minute, I'd be tempted to throw you in myself to be quite honest.

He laughs. He touches his face.

KILIAN. Christ. You've some left hook on ya, d'you know that?

Next morning. PAUDIE *is standing by the grave, drinking a can of beer.* KILIAN *enters.* PAUDIE *offers him the can.*

KILIAN. You havin' a laugh?

PAUDIE. Suit yerself.

PAUDIE *drinks.* KILIAN *lights a fag.*

Who put that plastic angel there?

KILIAN. Auntie Maureen I think.

PAUDIE (*leaning in to read inscription on angel*). 'Safe in the Arms of Jesus.' (*Pause.*) S'fuckin' well tacky.

KILIAN. I know.

PAUDIE. Looks like she bought it down the pound shop.

PAUDIE *drinks.* KILIAN *smokes.*

Got that song in my head.

KILIAN. What song?

PAUDIE *hums a bit of 'The Parting Glass'.*

PAUDIE. That one.

KILIAN. Yer singing's as bad as yer jokes.

PAUDIE. Did we play it last night?

KILIAN. Don't think so.

PAUDIE. Weird. It just… popped into my head. While I was stood here. (*Pause*.) D'you remember that lock-in that time? When he sang it? An' everyone went pure quiet. An' he made Big Billy Quirke cry. Bawling into his pint like a fuckin' baby.

KILIAN *gets a text on his phone. He reads it, replies quickly, then puts phone back in his pocket.*

KILIAN. Some head on me.

PAUDIE. How'd I get home?

KILIAN. Myself and Eilish walked ya.

PAUDIE. Did ya? I remember up to the point where I took a leak outside Mrs Reilly's place. But after that it's just a blur.

KILIAN. You aimed for her door.

PAUDIE. Ah she's a miserable old bitch.

KILIAN. Then you puked outside the GAA Club.

PAUDIE. What were we doin' down there?

KILIAN. You wanted to run naked on the pitch.

PAUDIE. Ah Jesus, tell me I didn't.

KILIAN. Eilish stopped you. Shame though, I was all for it.

PAUDIE. Was it a big puke?

KILIAN. Projectile. Then after that it was the church.

PAUDIE *looks at him blankly.*

You wanted to take down all the Stations of the Cross? An' then put them all back up again, 'cept in the wrong order?

PAUDIE. Bless me Father fer I have sinned. (*Pause.*) Drunk
walks into a confession box, sits down an' says nothin'. So
the priest clears his throat a bit, to get him started like. No
response. Priest coughs a few times. Total silence. So
eventually, the priest starts knockin' on the wall an' the
drunk pipes up an' says 'Ain't no use knockin', boy, there's
no paper this side neither.' (*Laughs.*) Eilish get home okay?

KILIAN. Think so, yeah.

PAUDIE. You think so?

KILIAN. I'm sure she did like.

PAUDIE. She was half-cut. Could be lying in a ditch
somewhere.

KILIAN. She's grand.

> PAUDIE *looks at* KILIAN. *Silence.* PAUDIE *drinks from the
> can.* KILIAN *gets another text on his phone. He doesn't look
> at it this time.*

PAUDIE. You just got a text there.

KILIAN. I know.

> *Pause.*

PAUDIE. Gonna see who it's from?

KILIAN. Not right now.

> *Silence.* KILIAN *stubs out his cigarette.* PAUDIE *finishes
> his beer, then scrunches up the can and throws it away.*

I *know* you're gonna pick that up.

> PAUDIE *rolls his eyes but picks it back up.*

Fuck's wrong with ya?

> KILIAN *lights another cigarette. Takes a few drags then
> passes it instinctively to* PAUDIE. PAUDIE *takes a long
> drag, then passes fag back to* KILIAN. *Silence. Then*
> PAUDIE *walks off.*

Where you / goin'?

PAUDIE. I need to clear my head. Alright? That fuckin' song's stuck in my head.

Kicks a stone on the ground.

Fuckin' stupid song.

He exits.

That afternoon. JIMMY's house. KILIAN's sitting by the fire reading a newspaper, looking very hungover now. We hear noises in the kitchen. Then a plate breaks.

KILIAN. You alright in there?

JIMMY (*voice offstage*). I'm grand!

KILIAN. Well you don't sound grand. You sound like yer trashin' the place.

JIMMY. Nearly done.

KILIAN. I told ya, I'm not drinkin' it!

JIMMY. You'll drink whatever the hell I bring ya to drink an' that'll be that!

JIMMY enters with a home-made hangover cure in a glass for KILIAN. He's more physically able than we last saw him.

An' yer lucky yer not in Outer Mongolia. They'd have ya swallowing sheeps' eyeballs. Here.

KILIAN. What is it?

JIMMY. Neveryoumind, just throw it back that big gob've yours an' be done.

KILIAN. It stinks.

JIMMY. Drink!

KILIAN throws it back and retches.

KILIAN. Jesus Christ, Jim!

JIMMY. Ah stop yer whinging. It's only a raw egg with a little Tabasco sauce. (*Sits down*.) He's back one day an' look at the state've ya.

KILIAN. We were celebrating.

JIMMY. Were ye now.

Pause.

KILIAN. So. Any news?

JIMMY. Well apart from the Queen droppin' by fer a cup've tea earlier, not much, no. Carol's comin' fer a visit next week though.

KILIAN. The niece-up-in-Dublin Carol?

JIMMY. Aye. With the eejit husband from Cork, who has somehow mysteriously developed a Dublin 4 accent. I mean, how does that happen unless you're a feckin' eejit. Likes to take charge Carol does. Her mother was the same. The eldest see. Thought it her divine right to boss the rest've us. Till I told her to feck off one day. (*Laughs*.) Well! She was sat on the swing in the garden lookin' at me, with her mouth wide open. Could've stuffed a cauliflower in there. You look green, boy.

KILIAN. Was that egg gone off?

JIMMY. Don't you dare get sick on my floor. Go get the basin.

KILIAN *exits to kitchen*. JIMMY *goes back to his paper*.

(*Tuts, then reads aloud*.) 'After the robbery, the terrified victim cycled for eight hours through the night to check himself into a nursing home, where he remains in care today.' He's only sixty-nine! Robbed him three nights in a row an' said they'd burn the house down if he told on 'em. Eight hours on a bike in the dead've night. We used leave the key in the door once. State've us.

KILIAN *re-enters with the basin*.

Walked past the Post Office yesterday. All boarded up. Been here since 1843 so it has. Ned's great-grandfather used run it. Important place y'know. Before all this email malarkey. An' the social faceworking.

KILIAN (*his head over the basin*). *Net*working.

JIMMY. Kept them sane so it did. What a thing to get a letter into your hands. The weight of it. The bit've perfume on the paper. Unions should be doin' somethin'!

KILIAN. Didn't that fella have a fuckload of money in the house by the way?

JIMMY. Well d'you know what they'd get?

KILIAN. I know, I know.

JIMMY *observes him for a few moments.*

JIMMY. How long you been coming to visit me, Kilian Óg?

KILIAN (*sitting up*). Good long while now, Jim.

JIMMY. Good long while now is right. Since you were a wee lad. You and Seamus. Back in the day when I still had the greyhounds. You'd come round to see the pups when they were small and bring Seamus with you. Ye used love the pups. An' I'd always have the few sweets out in the kitchen fer ye, wouldn't I?

KILIAN. You would, Jim. Is it not time fer your tablets?

JIMMY (*pointing to where they are.* KILIAN *gets the tablets*). An' one day, you brought along little Padraig O'Sullivan. Wanted to show him the pups too. Fierce excited you were altogether to be showing your friend the new pups.

KILIAN *hands him the pills and* JIMMY *swallows two.*

So I left ye to it an' when I came back, you were on yer own in the shed with two of the dogs asleep on yer lap. Happy out. 'Paudie needed the toilet, Jim,' you said. So I said grand and off I went to wash up and get the sweets. But when I come in, don't I hear a strange sort of rustling sound from in there – (*Points towards the kitchen.*) so I goes to investigate an' what was he doin'?

KILIAN. He was havin' a sweet.

JIMMY. He wasn't *havin'* a sweet! He was *stealin'* a sweet! Grubby little paw in the jar helping himself. Caught in the act as / one might say.

KILIAN. Ah c'mon, Jim, we were / kids.

JIMMY. An' what does the little thief do? He looks me straight in the eye. Straight in the eye, brazen like. I don't say a word only stare straight back. An' what does he do next? Well, doesn't he unwrap the sweet, stick it in his gob and saunter off outside. Saunter, mind. Not run. He didn't run. He *sauntered*.

JIMMY *looks at* KILIAN, *as if he's just explained the mysteries of the universe*.

KILIAN. Y'know, they should never've given him that loan in the first place.

JIMMY. He should never've taken it.

KILIAN. Everyone was takin' it!

JIMMY. I wasn't.

KILIAN. They were throwing / it away.

JIMMY. I never went to no / 'party'.

KILIAN. It was growing on the fuckin' trees / back then.

JIMMY (*reciting passionately*). 'For what died the sons of Róisín, was it greed? Was it greed that drove Wolfe Tone to a pauper's death in a cell of cold wet stone? Will German, French or Dutch inscribe the epitaph of Emmet? When we have sold enough of Ireland to be but strangers in it? For what died the sons of Róisín, was it *greed*?'

KILIAN (*beat*). God. You're fierce serious today.

KILIAN *puts his head back over the basin.* JIMMY *keeps his eyes on him.*

JIMMY. Leave Coolatully, boy. Before it's too late.

KILIAN. Christ's sake. Do I smell or / somethin'?

JIMMY. Hangin' round here on the dole with the likes of Padraig O'Sullivan'll get you nowhere.

KILIAN. Ah fer... anyway, I can't just magic up the cash. You need money to go. You need money to stay. You need money to take a shit in this world.

JIMMY. I'll give it you.

KILIAN. What?

JIMMY. The money.

KILIAN. Don't be stupid.

JIMMY. How much d'you need?

KILIAN. No.

JIMMY. Two thousand?

KILIAN. I'm not takin' nothin' off ya.

JIMMY. Three?

KILIAN. I'm not takin' yer money!

JIMMY. You listen here to me, who was it led his County out /
onto that –

KILIAN. Ah not / this again –

JIMMY. Listen to me! Who led his County out onto that pitch
for the 2004 Munster Minor Final when he was only
seventeen years old? Who was it scored the goal in injury
time with thirty seconds to go winning that game for the first
time in Coolatully Club history? Who was it they spoke about
for days and weeks and months afterwards, the story retold
again and again, 'bout how that boy was like a god on the
field that day? Why even Cúchulainn himself couldn't have
done it. Damn you. I won't stand by and watch / you rot now.

KILIAN. I can't leave the mam alone / with the bar.

JIMMY. Ah for God's sake! The woman's already lost one son.
D'you think she wants to lose another? *An dtuigeann tú?* [Do
you understand?]

Silence.

KILIAN. Who'd come to see you?

JIMMY. Carol wants to take me to Dublin.

KILIAN. Fer a holiday?

JIMMY. No, not fer a feckin' holiday.

KILIAN. Oh. Right.

JIMMY. Told her she'd have to drag me out an' strap me to the roof of the car so she would. But. When the time's right. I'm just… not a city man I s'pose. Spent time in London as a young fella y'know. Place was still in ruins back then. An' I worked on the Croydon flyover for nearly two years in the sixties. No machines. We cut those kerbs by hand. You could take the skin off if you weren't careful. No. Here's always been home for me. But. Things don't stay the same. We do what we have to do.

JIMMY *stokes the fire*.

KILIAN. They get earthquakes over there.

JIMMY. They get earthquakes off the coast've Cork, boy.

KILIAN. It's hot all the time. I'll burn up.

JIMMY. Use sunscreen. I've a bottle've the stuff out back.

KILIAN. Won't know no one.

JIMMY. What're you talkin' about, half've Ireland's already out there. Most of 'em since the 1600s.

KILIAN *puts his head in his hands*.

Take the money and go. (*Pause.*) You'll end up in that grave with your brother if you don't.

Silence. KILIAN *looks up at* JIMMY.

A nice cup've tea now I think, an' then we'll talk details.

KILIAN *exits to kitchen.* JIMMY *stokes the fire some more*.

Then we'll talk details.

That evening in the bar. KILIAN's *got his laptop out and is typing something.* PAUDIE *enters rubbing the back of his head.*

PAUDIE. I've just been assaulted.

KILIAN. What?

PAUDIE. Walloped round the back've the head.

KILIAN. Who?

PAUDIE. Mrs Reilly. I was passin' her gate an' this big hand comes out've nowhere like, an' whack! I actually saw stars.

KILIAN. Well, in fairness, you do have her a bit demented.

PAUDIE. She was hiding in the bushes like a mad one. I'd swear I saw her in camouflage. Anyway, wasn't it free fertilisation for the flowerbeds?

KILIAN. You were aiming for her door.

Pause. They laugh.

PAUDIE. I'd a good joke fer ya an' all. But I've it forgotten now. (*Pulling up a stool.*) I'm a gobshite.

KILIAN. You're not a gobshite.

PAUDIE. I am a gobshite.

KILIAN. Alright, you're a bit of a gobshite when you're drunk.

PAUDIE. I'm a massive gobshite when I'm drunk.

KILIAN. But in general you're alright.

PAUDIE. I just...

KILIAN. I know.

Silence.

PAUDIE. What's the plan then. You gonna try long-distance or something?

KILIAN. Hah?

PAUDIE. Well she's off to Australia, isn't she? Unless she's changed her mind.

KILIAN. No. She's going.

PAUDIE. So... how's it gonna work?

KILIAN. I dunno. I'm tryin' to figure stuff out.

PAUDIE. Like what? Christ. You're not gonna ask her to marry you, are ya?

KILIAN. No, ya feckin' eejit.

PAUDIE. Thank fuck. 'Cause I'd have to say something then. I'd have to step in and sort it out then like, y'know? (*Pause*.) Ah for fuck's sake, Kil, what is it?

   KILIAN *opens something on the laptop and turns it round so* PAUDIE *can see the screen*. PAUDIE *reads*.

   'Specialising in large industrial construction, this client currently has a number of long-term projects underway across... Sydney's Western suburbs.' (*Looks at* KILIAN.) Sydney Australia?

KILIAN. No. Sydney Ireland.

   Beat. Then PAUDIE *starts whooping and hollering in delight*.

   Shut up, man, the mam's upstairs taking a nap!

PAUDIE. I knew you'd cave! I fuckin' knew it! It'll take a while to get the cash together like. We'll need at least two grand between visas an' flights an' stuff. Each. More if there's agency fees. How much you got?

KILIAN. Not much. But / that's –

PAUDIE. Alright, not a problem. Specially if we get jobs sorted first. I can ask the old man. Might lend me something. And your mam, maybe you could ask her? It'll take a while like. A good year at least / I'd say but –

KILIAN. Jimmy's giving me the money.

PAUDIE. What?

KILIAN. Jimmy Barrett. He's giving me the money.

PAUDIE. What, he's just... giving you a few grand. Just like that?

KILIAN. He thinks I should go. He's been on at me for months.

PAUDIE. Huh. Well. Owes you a few grand in carer bills by now anyway I s'pose.

KILIAN. He's an old family friend.

PAUDIE. Still owes you.

KILIAN. He owes me nothin'.

Pause.

PAUDIE. Alright. Good. Great. So I just need to sort myself out then. It's January now. I could have it by… Christmas? Yeah. Yeah I could have it by then, I'm sure I can / sort something.

KILIAN. He says I have to go by the summer.

PAUDIE. Hah?

KILIAN. I have to go by then or the deal's off. Wants me to get on with it. Thinks I'll change my mind.

They look at each other.

PAUDIE. Any chance of a pint?

KILIAN *pulls him a pint.* PAUDIE *drinks.*

KILIAN. I'm sorry.

PAUDIE. For what?

KILIAN. For…

Silence. Then PAUDIE *raises his glass and bursts into song –*

PAUDIE. 'Oh all the comrades that e'er I've had, are sorry for my going away…'

KILIAN. Fuckin' eejit.

PAUDIE. Forget the words now. (*Improvises.*) 'So fill the glass with lots of beer, an' go get shit-faced in Oz fer me.'

They laugh. PAUDIE *salutes and drinks.*

D'you remember the time I nicked those sweets? He's had it in for me since then. Which is a bit unfair really. I mean, I was a kid. An' you didn't mind stuffin' your face with half the loot if I remember correctly. (*Pause*.) Fair play to him though. Take the money. I'll bate the head off you if you don't.

KILIAN *laughs a little*.

An' I'll not be long after ya anyway.

KILIAN. Yeah.

PAUDIE. Not stayin' here to rot on the dole.

KILIAN. I can do the groundwork.

PAUDIE. Finished with Coolatully.

KILIAN. I'll collect you at the airport.

PAUDIE. Dead in the water here.

Silence. PAUDIE *drinks*.

So. Jimmy must have a bit've moolah, then, hah?

KILIAN. S'pose.

PAUDIE. Bit've cash? Bit've a hoard stashed away in that little cottage of his? Makes sense. Old bachelor like him. No kids. Didn't he get some inheritance a few years back as well?

KILIAN. Think so, yeah.

PAUDIE. I remember hearing 'bout that. Some spinster cousin over in America. Left him a small fortune apparently.

KILIAN. Remember hearing 'bout it but… he never said much.

PAUDIE. Well, you wouldn't, would you. You'd keep that to yourself if you'd any sense. Specially an aul fella like Jimmy. Bet he keeps all his money under his bed or somethin'. (*Pause*.) He does, doesn't he!

KILIAN. What?

PAUDIE. He keeps all his money under his bed!

KILIAN. How would I know!

PAUDIE. Course you know.

KILIAN. Why you so interested?

PAUDIE. I'm not fuckin' interested, I'm / just sayin'.

KILIAN. Well you sound interested to me.

Pause.

PAUDIE. What're you implying there, Kil?

KILIAN. Nothin'.

They look at each other.

PAUDIE. I walked into an empty church hall and robbed a tin've money. It was for my car loan. 'Cause I needed my car. Anyway, it was just fuckin' sittin' there. Practically asking for it. But I don't go round robbing old pensioners. You know that. You of all people. (*Beat.*) An' I didn't fuckin' know it was money for sick kids neither. Thought it was… to fix the fuckin' roof or somethin'.

KILIAN. Sorry.

PAUDIE. Fuck off.

Silence. PAUDIE drinks.

KILIAN. Can't think straight any more. Sometimes I feel… like I can't breathe. Like it's all been for nothin'. Every moment, every day, it all means nothin'. An' it makes my chest go tight. S'like I'm stood on the edge of something. Like I'm… stood on the edge.

Silence. PAUDIE notices KILIAN's CV on the laptop.

PAUDIE. Make the font smaller, get it down to two pages. An' add a personal statement here. You know, what you can bring to the role, why you're the one to hire, blah blah. They always say do that down the Jobcentre. Hey. You listening to me?

They look at each other for a moment.

Are ya?

KILIAN *nods*.

Good.

February

EILISH *and* KILIAN *are sitting on a sand dune. The light is dimming. We can hear the sound of waves throughout the scene.*

EILISH. Stretch in the day now. The light lasts for longer.

KILIAN. I'll miss this.

EILISH. There's beaches out there y'know.

KILIAN. Yeah but… not like this.

EILISH. No. Better.

Pause.

KILIAN. Paudie's in a slump.

Pause.

EILISH. D'you remember the time Seamus found the nest down here? That day we dossed off?

KILIAN. Yeah.

EILISH. An' you and Paudie had that row?

KILIAN. 'Cause he picked the eggs up. You never pick the eggs up.

EILISH. Ye wouldn't talk the rest've the day.

KILIAN. They abandon the nest when that happens.

EILISH. Next morning ye still weren't talking, an' we were all called up to the office an' Sister Clancy tore strips off us.

KILIAN. Fuckin' demon that one.

EILISH. Mostly Paudie though. Yelling at him. All up in his face. Her spit in his eye. Then next thing, you start yelling back. Told her she'd an awful fuckin' manner on her an' she needed to loosen up a bit, maybe her veil was too tight. (*Laughs.*) Her eyes bulged when you said that. About the veil. Ended up in detention a week longer than us. You and Paudie are solid. Always have been. Always will be. (*Pause.*) The sun'll be nice. Rains there too like. But more sun than rain.

KILIAN. Are they still a colony?

EILISH. What? No. The Queen's Head of State or something, but they're definitely not still a colony.

KILIAN. Why's she Head of State then?

EILISH. I dunno. Just worked out that way.

KILIAN. Still under the thumb then if you ask me.

EILISH. There's these walks you can do. Round Bondi Beach. One takes you past the most scenic graveyard in the whole world.

KILIAN. Lovely.

EILISH. Irish Fenian buried there. Michael… something or other.

KILIAN. Narrows it down.

EILISH. There he is with all the famous poets and Prime Ministers. Up on the cliffs overlooking the sea. (*Pause.*) Have you started?

KILIAN. What?

EILISH. Packing?

KILIAN. No.

EILISH. Why?

KILIAN. Sure what do I have to pack? Few T-shirts an' a pair've jeans? Take me all've five minutes.

EILISH. S'pose. I started weeks ago.

KILIAN. Bit soon isn't it?

EILISH. 'Bout ten suitcases at first.

KILIAN. Yer not headin' out fer another while yet.

EILISH. Then I thought, d'you know what, I don't need all this. So I got it down to three last week. Now I'm on two.

KILIAN. Gonna put the rest in storage?

EILISH. Why would I do that? Sure I'm not comin' back.

KILIAN. Not even for Christmas?

EILISH. Let's think about this for a minute. Christmas back here in this shithole in the freezin' fuckin' cold an' the pourin' rain, or a barbecue in the sun on the most famous beach in the world.

KILIAN. Yer on a one-way ticket then?

EILISH. Aren't you?

Pause.

KILIAN. Still not comfortable 'bout the earthquakes.

EILISH. Oh my God, you'd swear you were Charlton Heston in *Earthquake* or something. D'you even know anything about earthquakes? An' by the way, there was one off the coast of Wexford last month. Knocked a tree over. Rattled a few doors even. And there was one in North Clare in 2010. Some thought it was a / meteorite.

KILIAN. I hear Ron's in Sydney now too. I swear to God, if we go halfway round the world an' I end up bumping into that fucker I'm booking the next / flight back.

EILISH. Look, come if you want. Or not. I don't give a shit either way.

KILIAN. What're you talkin' about? Course I'm comin'. I was jokin'.

Silence.

The mam wants to plant a tree.

EILISH. Wha?

KILIAN. She wants to plant a tree fer him. On the day.

Pause.

EILISH. What kinda tree?

KILIAN. Oak. Keep tellin' her the garden isn't big enough. In a few years it'll've taken up all the space. (*Pause.*) Father Ryan's gonna say a mass in the bar.

EILISH. Don't like him. He's too fat. I don't trust fat priests.

KILIAN. First anniversary. Mad that is. Pure mad.

Silence. She shivers.

EILISH. I think I might just set fire to it all.

KILIAN. Hah?

EILISH. My stuff. Might just have a big ol' bonfire in the back garden an' burn the lot of it. Cook a few sausages fer the dinner while I'm at it. Get some practice in.

Sound of waves.

April

The 17th – two days before the first anniversary.

Late morning. PAUDIE *is sitting by the grave with a can of beer. It's the first of a six-pack lying on the ground beside him in a blue carrier bag. A heavy fog hangs in the air and a solitary bird sings intermittently.*

PAUDIE. Dirty old day. Fog in April. Feels more like January. D'you know what this place is like now? It's like the fuckin' set for *Children of Men*, that's what it's like. (*Drinks.*) Remember John Cooney? Friend of the old man up in Dublin? Fella with the security firm? He used come down here fer his holidays. He'd take us fishing. D'you remember? We'd all be bored stiff, 'cept fer the time Kil got the line caught in his pants. An' we used call him Looney Cooney behind his back, 'cept he heard you one day, ya big muppet, an' that was the end of the fishing trips. Anyway. Said he could sort me out with a job maybe. The old man thinks I should go. Can you imagine? A security guard? 'Oi, lads! No ID, no entry.' Sure they're all just rejects from the Gardaí or the army, s'why they're all so fuckin' miserable all the time. He can piss off if he thinks I'm goin' up there to be a fuckin' security guard fer the rest've my life. (*Drinks.*) They call it 'County Bondi' now. Even sell Barry's Tea out there. And Tayto's.

KILIAN *enters.*

KILIAN. Alright.

PAUDIE. Alright, man.

KILIAN. Dirty old day, hah?

PAUDIE. Meant to clear a bit by the end've the week.

> *He offers him a can.* KILIAN *shakes his head and lights a cigarette.*

KILIAN. Thought you had a thing down the Jobcentre today?

PAUDIE. Fuck it. Waste've time. (*Imitating interview.*) 'So. Mr O'Sullivan. What were you doing from last July to the beginning of January this year?' 'Ermm, I was in prison.' 'Really?' 'Yeah. For stealing charity money from a church hall.' 'Right.' 'Money for the kids.' 'Oh?' 'Sick ones.'

> *He grins a big grin at imaginary interviewer.*

KILIAN (*passing the cigarette*). You didn't know what the money was for.

PAUDIE. God I miss that car. Fuck's sake. (*Beat.*) Still, could be worse, could be in a gulag in North Korea.

> *They laugh.*

> PAUDIE *passes cigarette back and drinks.* KILIAN *smokes.*

> *Silence.*

Bird's stopped.

KILIAN. Hah?

PAUDIE. There was a bird singin' a minute ago. (*Pause.*) Don't feel like a year. (*Pause.*) On your way to Jim's?

KILIAN. Yeah. The niece is down again.

PAUDIE. The one married to that gobshite?

KILIAN. That's the one.

PAUDIE. Met him once. At the County Fair. On about rugby the whole time. An' his stock investments. (*Dublin 4 voice.*) 'All depends on the rate of return, Padraig.'

KILIAN. '*Padraig*'?

PAUDIE. 'Rate of return and market bubbles.' I was so fuckin'
bored I could've clawed my own face off.

They laugh.

PAUDIE *drinks.* KILIAN *smokes.*

Silence.

KILIAN. Sometimes I wish it was me in there.

PAUDIE *immediately punches him in the arm.*

Ow!

PAUDIE. What kind've a fuckin' stupid thing's that to say?

Pause.

KILIAN. He came to my room. That night. Like he used do
years back when he was small. He came to my room an' he
sat on my bed an' we talked. For ages. The mam had to
knock on the wall twice to tell us to shut the fuck up we were
laughin' so loud. Stupid stuff. Messin' like. Till I couldn't
keep my eyes open. An' I thought, sure he's grand. He's fine
now again. 'A good laugh an' a long sleep, Kil. The two best
cures.' He said that just before he left. A good laugh an' a
long sleep. (*Pause.*) Never even heard the engine start up.

Silence.

PAUDIE. GAA Clubs out in Sydney y'know. Should hook up
with one. Best midfielder for miles you were. I'd love to
have made the team. Never good enough though. Not like
you and Seamy. Ye were magic. I was always left watchin'
on the sidelines, hah?

KILIAN *smokes.*

KILIAN. What'll you do if…

Pause.

PAUDIE. D'you remember Looney Cooney? Told the old fella
he might be able to sort me out.

KILIAN. A security guard?

PAUDIE. Yeah.

KILIAN. What, like… standin' round Lidl's all day?

PAUDIE. It's a fuckin' job, isn't it?

Pause.

KILIAN. This isn't even our mess. Makes me want to put my fist through a wall.

PAUDIE. Then you'd have a broken fist.

Silence. They're both looking at the grave.

Even a lottery win wouldn't give us what we need.

KILIAN. What's that?

PAUDIE. A fuckin' purpose. S'what it's all about. Feeling useful. A job makes you somebody. Work makes you somebody. You can't be a somebody without it.

KILIAN. If I'd enough cash for the both / of us –

PAUDIE. I know.

KILIAN. You'll be out there yourself before long.

PAUDIE. Yeah.

KILIAN. You will, man.

PAUDIE. What's the definition of optimism?

KILIAN. Hah?

PAUDIE. The definition of optimism?

KILIAN. I dunno. What?

PAUDIE. Investment banker ironing five shirts on a Sunday night.

KILIAN. Funny.

PAUDIE. Hilarous.

Silence.

KILIAN. I'd better go.

PAUDIE. Tell old Jimmy I said hello.

KILIAN. You callin' by the pub later?

PAUDIE. Yeah. Fer a change.

KILIAN. Right. Well. See ya there then.

PAUDIE (*saluting*). See ya.

> KILIAN *stops at the gate and watches* PAUDIE *open up another can of beer. Then he exits.*

A little later. JIMMY*'s house. There's no one home. Someone knocks on the door. Pause. Another knock.*

KILIAN. Jimmy? You in? (*Pause.*) Jim?

> *A key turns in the lock and* KILIAN *enters quickly. He's half-expecting to find* JIMMY *on the floor. Relieved, he closes the door after him.*

Jim?

He remembers something.

Shit. Lunch with Carol.

He walks off into kitchen for a few moments. We hear a window being closed. He re-enters, finds a scrap of paper and writes a quick note, reading out loud as he writes:

'Called round. Forgot about lunch thing. You left window open AGAIN.'

Places note on JIMMY*'s chair. He looks around the room, making sure there's nothing to be cleaned or tidied up. He spots the hurley stick standing against the wall. He picks it up and swings it gently back and forth for a moment. Pause. Then he throws an imaginary sliotar into the air and skillfully knocks it down the field. He plays out the end of a big final, imitating a commentator's voice. He speaks rapidly but plays out the action in slow motion –*

Thirty seconds left in this All-Ireland Hurling Final. Kilian Óg coming away with the ball to the far side chased by that big prick Ronald O'Callaghan. Still going. Still going. Still going. Óg passes to O'Sullivan. O'Sullivan passes back. Óg presses on. He throws. He strikes – IT'S OVER THE BAR! He's lifted the sides at Croke Park! Coolatully win by one point! A beautiful point! They needed a lifeline and by God they got one! (*Imitates huge crowd cheering.*)

Silence. He gets a text alert. He drops the hurley stick and checks the phone. He texts back quickly, then stoops down to pick up the hurley stick and put it back in its place. He pauses. The stick is lying on the spot where JIMMY *keeps his money. He stares at it for a long time, thinking, running things through in his mind. He makes a decision, kneels down and takes up the floorboard. He reaches in and lifts out a biscuit tin, opens it and stuffs the cash into his jacket. He closes the tin and puts it back, replaces the floorboard and stands up. Silence. He bends down again and pulls the floorboard back up, takes out the biscuit tin and leaves it open on the floor. Quickly, he walks back out to kitchen. We hear the sound of the window being reopened.* KILIAN *re-enters. He turns the stool over. He takes some letters and newspapers from a small side table and scatters them on the floor. He replaces the hurley stick and walks to the door. He stops, and for a moment we think he might be about to change his mind. Then he exits abruptly without looking back.*

The note is still on the chair.

The door locks behind him.

Silence.

A few hours later. Early evening. PAUDIE *is sitting on the beach. He still has his blue bag of cans and is on the last one. The light is dimming. His hood is up. We can hear the sound of waves.* KILIAN *enters in very good form.*

KILIAN. Alright.

PAUDIE. Alright.

> KILIAN *sits down beside him.*

> You on a break?

KILIAN. Mam's taken over. Dead in there. Big Billy Quirke, Paddy Brody Junior and a Jack Russell.

PAUDIE. He's a little shit that Jack Russell. Nips at your heels. I swear to God, I'll throw him through a window one've these days. The mam up an' about then?

KILIAN. Yeah.

PAUDIE. That's good.

> PAUDIE *passes can to* KILIAN *who gulps half it down in one go.*

KILIAN. I've a thirst on me.

PAUDIE. No shit.

> KILIAN *hands the can back and lights a cigarette. They pass the cigarette back and forth between them.*

> Fuckin' freezin'.

KILIAN. Siberian. Come back to the pub.

PAUDIE. Nah. I'm grand here a while. Seriously, me an' that Jack Russell really don't get on. (*Pause.*) You're very… cheerful.

KILIAN. Am I?

PAUDIE. Yeah. You drunk?

KILIAN. Don't always need to be drunk to be happy.

PAUDIE. No, but it helps. (*Drinks.*) I'll look in on her y'know.

KILIAN. Hah?

PAUDIE. Your mam. When you're gone. I'll keep an eye on her. Help out in the bar even. If I'm not doin' anythin' else like. You sure you're not drunk? 'Cause there's a vibe off ya.

KILIAN *takes a thickish envelope out of his jacket pocket and passes it to* PAUDIE. KILIAN *smokes*. PAUDIE *opens envelope and looks inside*.

Jesus.

KILIAN. There'll be no lookin' in on my mam. We're sorted. S'for your visa.

PAUDIE. My… what?

KILIAN. An' you can forget about Lidl's an' all.

PAUDIE. Where the fuck d'you get it?

KILIAN. Does it matter? Just take it. We're going. All three of us. Christmas down the beach this year!

PAUDIE. I can't take it.

KILIAN. What?

PAUDIE. There's a couple've grand in here!

KILIAN. Take the money, Paudie. It's for your visa!

PAUDIE. You fuckin' robbed it, didn't you?

KILIAN. No.

PAUDIE. Don't fuckin' lie to me, do I look like an idiot? You robbed it. Didn't ya?

Pause.

KILIAN. Pot, kettle an' all that.

PAUDIE *punches* KILIAN *in the arm*.

Owww! Would you stop hittin' me!

PAUDIE. Think I'm proud, hah? Stealing cash from a church hall like a fuckin' scumbag? You think I'm proud've that? (*Pause.*) Oh Jesus. Tell me you didn't. (*Pause.*) Fuck. You did, didn't you. This is Jimmy Barrett's money, isn't it. (*Stands up and looks down on* KILIAN.) Are you on drugs or something!

KILIAN. What's wrong with ya?!

PAUDIE. What's wrong with me? What's wrong wi–... I don't even have a fuckin' alibi! I've been down here most've the day! I might as well throw myself into the cell right now an' be done with it, *that's* what's fuckin' wrong with me, you big fuckin' eejit!

KILIAN. I... I...

PAUDIE. D'you've any idea what that place is like? Do ya? I can still hear the clanging doors, man. There's fuckin' metal everywhere, the food is shit an' d'you even know what a shiv is? Well I'll tell ya what a shiv is, it's a fuckin' knife made from a toothbrush. A *knife* made from / a *toothbrush*!

KILIAN. Alright! I wasn't thinking straight!

PAUDIE. No shit, Sherlock.

KILIAN. I... I just... Jimmy'll be alright. But you're not alright. You're not / alright, Paudie.

PAUDIE. No, *you're* not alright! What's next, Kilian? Some post office somewhere? Fuckin' ransom money?

KILIAN (*standing up*). Look at you! With your empty six-pack and your eyes hangin' out've your / head!

PAUDIE (*holding up envelope*). What's that got to do with this!

KILIAN. EVERYTHING! FUCKIN' EVERYTHING! OKAY?

Pause.

PAUDIE. Take it back.

KILIAN. It's for your / visa.

PAUDIE. I said take / it back.

KILIAN. An' I said it's for / your visa.

PAUDIE. Ah fer fuck's sake, we both know the record's gonna stop me!

KILIAN. But you said six months won't be / a problem.

PAUDIE. Technically. Won't stop some bollox in an office somewhere stamping 'Application Denied' in bright-red ink if that's what he wants to do though, will it? I mean, what the hell do I know? I lie to myself. I lie to myself 'cause it keeps me sane.

They look at each other.

I'll be hung for this. They'll all think it's me. All the fuckin' fingers will be pointing straight at me. Mrs Reilly'll have a field day.

KILIAN. I... I just didn't think.

PAUDIE. No, Einstein, you didn't. (*Forces the envelope into* KILIAN*'s hand*.) Take it back.

He exits. KILIAN *just stares at the envelope.*

Next day. Late morning. JIMMY *is sitting in his front room. Immediately we know that something's changed. He looks pale and drawn, like he's aged ten years. The hurley stick lies across his lap. There's a knock on the door. He jumps a little.*

JIMMY. Carol?

KILIAN. It's me, Jim.

Pause.

JIMMY. Use yer key.

KILIAN *unlocks the door and enters.*

Put the heart crossways on me there.

KILIAN. Sorry. You on yer own?

JIMMY. Carol's gone to the town for a few things. Wanted me to come but...

KILIAN *sits down.*

So you know?

KILIAN. Whole village knows.

JIMMY. Front-page news, hah?

KILIAN. Parish newsletter at least.

JIMMY smiles.

I'm sorry, Jim.

JIMMY. Must've been a rake've a thing. That window's small. Narrow. A squirrel couldn't fit through it. I tell you though, if I'd been here. (*Clutches the stick tightly.*) If I'd been here.

KILIAN. I'm glad you weren't.

JIMMY. D'you notice anything?

KILIAN. Hah?

JIMMY. When you called round?

KILIAN. When?

JIMMY. Yesterday. What's wrong with ya. D'you get a bang on the head or something? You left a note. 'Bout the window.

The colour drains from KILIAN's face as JIMMY takes the note from his pocket.

KILIAN. Oh yeah. Yeah. I... I forgot about that. Yeah. I called round alright. 'Cept you were out.

JIMMY. Lunch. With Carol.

KILIAN. Yeah. Yeah I forgot 'bout the lunch.

JIMMY. I had the salmon. Funny colour though. Carol thinks it was reconstituted.

KILIAN. Found the window open alright, so I closed it fer ya.

JIMMY. An' ya didn't notice nothin'?

KILIAN. No. No. Not that I can remember.

JIMMY. Must've been after your visit so.

KILIAN. Yeah. Must've been. They must've... forced it or somethin'.

JIMMY. Must've. (*Puts the note back in his pocket.*) S'where they stick bits've leftover salmon together an' dye it pink. (*Pause.*) They could be back for more.

KILIAN. They won't.

JIMMY. How d'you know? Should never've closed that station. Bunch've lunatics runnin' the country. Didn't take it all see? Could've taken it all. Strange. (*Pause*.) I got Carol to mop the floors after. (*To himself, amazed*.) We used leave the key in the door.

KILIAN. Can I get you anything, Jim?

JIMMY. Fastest fieldsport on earth. An' played for honour so it is, not money, but honour. Mighty game. You should be out playing. A fine player you were once. A fine player once, / Kilian Óg.

KILIAN. Would'ya stop goin' on about the fuckin' hurling, Jim. I just... I just don't play any more alright?

Pause.

JIMMY. Aye. Things don't stay the same I s'pose.

KILIAN. Will I... will I turn on the radio?

JIMMY. Batteries are dead.

KILIAN. Oh.

JIMMY. What's wrong with ya. Look like you need to snap a branch in two. (*Silence. Leans back in his chair*.) You'd miss the old *raidió*. (*Starts singing a little of 'Come Back to Stay'*.) They used play that in the dance hall in Cricklewood. An' we all there clingin' to each other. Smell of Silvikrin in the air. An' beer an' floor polish. An' a fierce longing.

KILIAN. Will I make some tea, Jim?

JIMMY. I'm shittin' an' pissin' like a baby. Carol says it's the nerves.

Silence. KILIAN *clears up a few newspapers. We see the guilt starting to eat at him*.

It wasn't forced by the way.

KILIAN. Hah?

JIMMY. The window. It wasn't forced. But I said to Carol, I said maybe he just didn't close it proper.

KILIAN. I mustn't have.

JIMMY. You mustn't have, no. Carol wanted to tell the Guards. 'Bout the note. I said sure what d'you want to do that for? That's only confusin' things. Sure he'd nothin' to do with it. He'd hardly leave a note if he'd somethin' to do with it, he's not a pure eejit.

KILIAN. Can I… will I bring in some briquettes?

Long pause.

JIMMY. Real peat fire back then. They used make a little circle round here. Once the work was done. An' the prayers said. Real peat. With the crackle an' smoke an' little sparks rising up into the night. I remember the feet. And the faces. The big strong weather-beaten faces lookin' down, winking at me, knowin' I should've been in bed long ago but sayin' nothin'. My stomach would go quare then with the excitement as I settled under the legs of some neighbour or other come in fer the warmth an' the chat. An' save fer the blowin' of the wind o'er the cliffs out there, a hush would fall over us in here. Like a spell. An' we all starin' at the dancin' flames, seeing shapes an' figures jumpin' out at us. Waiting fer them. Fer the stories. 'Bout times past an' folk long gone from this world. So vivid they'd have you leapin' away at a falling leaf on your way home in the dark. I used love those stories. An' those people. Huddled together in the glow of the fire.

Pause.

KILIAN. Have you taken your medicine today?

JIMMY. *Ní fhanann rudaí mar a chéile go deo.* [Things don't stay the same for ever.]

KILIAN. Jim?

JIMMY. Hah?

KILIAN. Have you taken your medicine?

JIMMY. Aye. (*Pause.*) Carol thinks a change of scenery might do me good. But I'm not the city type.

KILIAN. I'm so sorry, Jim.

JIMMY. Used be a time you'd tip your hat an' say good morning. Now they walk round with their eyes cast down. (*Pause*.) Why are you sorry? (*Pause*.) Why are you sorry, Kilian Óg?

KILIAN. I… I'm just sorry for you. For what happened. I'm sorry for you, Jim.

JIMMY *leans forward in his chair.*

JIMMY. Where was he?

KILIAN. What?

JIMMY. Where was he?

KILIAN. Down by the grave. He was down by the grave with me. I swear on my life he was.

JIMMY. You tell him from me. You tell him from me that I was a strong man once. That I broke rocks with my bare hands once. An' I swear, if I ever see him again, if I ever so much as set eyes / on him again.

KILIAN. It wasn't / him, Jimmy!

JIMMY. I'll kill him! I'll put my two hands round his neck an' / snap it in two!

KILIAN. Jimmy, stop it. Yer gonna make / yerself ill.

JIMMY. I'll put him in the ground so I will, an' all the rest of them, God damn them to hell. God damn them all to hell! (*Goes pale and dizzy for a moment*.)

KILIAN. Jim? Jim, you alright?

Pause. JIMMY *collects himself.*

JIMMY. Down by the grave you say?

KILIAN. I swear to God.

JIMMY. You spend too much time down there, boy. (*Pause. To himself*.) Met a young lady once. She wore her hair up. Pinned at the sides with little strands falling loose. An' her eyes were green. But I had to go away. No work see, so I had to go and build the roads. Her letters always smelled like roses.

JIMMY *leans back in his chair and closes his eyes. Silence.*

KILIAN. My visa came through. Jim?

JIMMY opens his eyes.

My visa came through.

JIMMY just nods, then closes his eyes again.

Are you tired, Jim?

JIMMY. Slept bad last night.

KILIAN. You should rest a while then.

JIMMY. Could feel the dip in the bed.

KILIAN. Go and lie down.

JIMMY. An' there was a fierce kind've chill in the air.

KILIAN. I'll stay till Carol gets back.

JIMMY. She'll be back soon. (*Stands up using the hurley stick to support him as he moves. Looks at the floorboard for a moment.*) If I'd been here. I tell you.

KILIAN. Go on, Jim.

JIMMY. They would've got a crack've this.

KILIAN. I'll stay till Carol gets back. Go on away and / have a –

JIMMY. STOP TELLING ME WHAT TO DO.

KILIAN hangs his head.

Have me all confused.

Silence.

I… a sleep'll do me good. A nice long sleep. (*Exits, taking hurley stick with him.*) I'm just very tired today.

Silence. KILIAN takes the envelope out of his jacket pocket and stares at it. A loud thud comes from bedroom offstage.

KILIAN. Jim? Jimmy? Fuck.

KILIAN races out to JIMMY, putting envelope back in his jacket pocket as he exits.

Later that night. PAUDIE and KILIAN are sitting in the pub. It's just before midnight and the curtains are drawn. The envelope is lying on the bar. KILIAN sniffs at his jumper.

KILIAN. I can smell that hospital.

PAUDIE. I can smell that Jack Russell. You should make them wash it. Stinking up the furniture.

Footsteps move around upstairs. PAUDIE looks up.

That your mam? Course it's your mam. Who else would it be.

Footsteps die away. Silence.

His health wasn't good anyway.

KILIAN pours another drink and knocks it back in one go. Pause. Then he flings the glass against the wall. It shatters.

Your mam'll have heard that. (*Pause.*) Look. They've nothin' on me. They were just makin' enquiries. They called to all the neighbours.

KILIAN hits himself hard in the head.

Stop it.

KILIAN hits himself again.

Stop it, you fuckin' lunatic.

KILIAN starts hitting himself over and over, losing control.

Pull yourself together, man!

PAUDIE grabs hold of him, restraining him.

Jesus Christ!

KILIAN. Couldn't look him in the eye.

PAUDIE. That's 'cause you've a conscience!

KILIAN. He knew.

PAUDIE. He didn't know.

KILIAN. He knew!

PAUDIE. It's not your fault! An' keep yer fuckin' voice down, you'll wake your mam.

KILIAN. Whose fault is it then, Paudie? Hah? Whose fault is it? The bankers?

PAUDIE. Well, now you mention / it …

KILIAN. The government?

PAUDIE. Keep yer voice / down.

KILIAN. That asshole down the Jobcentre?

PAUDIE. Which one?

KILIAN. Ron O'Callaghan? Hah? That prick Ronald O'Callaghan, is it his fault? Or Tom Moriarty maybe? How 'bout Sister / Clancy? Mrs Reilly?

PAUDIE. I'm gettin' tired've / this.

KILIAN. Seamus then. Is it his fault? Well? Is it?

Silence. It starts raining outside.

PAUDIE. Sit the fuck down.

KILIAN *sits.* PAUDIE *goes behind the bar and gets him a glass of water. He puts it down in front of him. Then he goes and gets a little brush and pan and starts brushing up the broken shards of glass.*

You need sleep. Hospitals suck the life out of people.

KILIAN. I'm so stupid.

PAUDIE. Yer not stupid.

KILIAN. I left the note there.

PAUDIE (*stops sweeping*). Hah?

KILIAN. I'd left him a note. 'Bout the window bein' open.

PAUDIE. An' ya left it there?

KILIAN. I forgot about it.

PAUDIE. A note?

KILIAN. Yes! A note! I left him a note!

PAUDIE (*pause. Then goes back to sweeping*). Yeah, well that *was* stupid.

KILIAN. I forgot / about it.

PAUDIE. That was pretty fuckin' stupid / alright.

KILIAN. I told him I mustn't have closed it properly. He said 'you mustn't / have, no.'

PAUDIE. To be honest, that's probably the most stupid thing you've ever done in your life. Ever. Fuck!

KILIAN. What?

PAUDIE. Splinter. (*Sucks his finger.*) Shit. S'gone right in. D'you've a needle?

KILIAN. Yeah, hang on there, I'll just grab my sewing kit.

PAUDIE (*manages to grip the splinter between his nails*). Hang on. Here we go. (*Starts pulling it out.*) Oh fuck that stings that stings that really really stings... gotcha! Ya little fucker! (*Sucks his finger. Notices* KILIAN *looking at him.*) What?

KILIAN. Big baby.

PAUDIE. They can kill ya.

KILIAN. No they can't.

PAUDIE. They fuckin' can.

KILIAN. Old wives' tale.

PAUDIE. They get into the heart.

KILIAN. That's bullshit.

PAUDIE. Into the heart an' then yer dead. So. Stop breakin' stuff. (*Pause.*) Look. He'd never think it was you. Okay? Never. You just weren't thinking straight. Obviously. Leaving a fuckin' note there I mean / c'mon.

There's a knock on the door.

EILISH. Kilian?

KILIAN. Fuck.

She knocks again.

EILISH. Kilian? You in there?

PAUDIE. Go on, man. It's dark. An' it's pissing it down.

KILIAN goes to the door, unlocks it and lets her in.

EILISH. Your phone's off. I was worried.

He can't look her in the eye.

PAUDIE. Watch your step there, Eilish. Glass on the floor.

EILISH. What happened?

PAUDIE. Yer man here had a moment. But he's grand now. Aren't ya?

KILIAN. Yeah.

EILISH. How is he?

PAUDIE. They're monitoring his heart or something.

KILIAN. Strapped to a drip. He hates needles.

PAUDIE. But he's grand. The doctor said he just needs rest. To build his strength back up. It was the shock y'know?

EILISH. Yeah.

PAUDIE. He'll be out in no time.

Pause.

EILISH. Wonder if we know them.

PAUDIE. My bet's on Mrs Reilly.

EILISH. I mean, what you did was wrong. But you just walked into an empty church hall and took some cash. It was wrong like but… you didn't break into some old man's home. That's different. What if he'd been there? Fuckin' cowards whoever they are.

Silence.

PAUDIE. Why do scuba divers always fall backwards off their boats? 'Cause if they fell forwards they'd still be in the feckin' boat!

Nobody laughs except PAUDIE. *Pause.* PAUDIE *notices the envelope is still on the bar.*

D'you want a drink, Eilish?

EILISH. Some water. Thanks.

PAUDIE *gets up to fetch a glass. He tries to move a newspaper so that it covers the envelope.* KILIAN *stops his hand.*

KILIAN. Leave it.

PAUDIE. Ah, Kil, would ya / just –

KILIAN. I said leave it. (*Looks at* EILISH.) Open it.

PAUDIE (*to* EILISH). Don't.

KILIAN. Open it.

EILISH. This?

KILIAN. Yeah.

EILISH *takes the envelope and looks inside. Then she looks at* KILIAN.

Know where that came from?

She shakes her head.

Want me to tell you?

She shakes her head.

That's Jimmy Barrett's money that is.

EILISH *looks at* PAUDIE.

PAUDIE. Oh – thanks!

KILIAN. Don't look at him.

She looks back at KILIAN. *Then she places the envelope back on the bar. Nobody moves or says anything for a long time.*

EILISH. Have you gone mad?

PAUDIE. He wasn't thinkin' straight. He's givin' it back.

EILISH. Why?

PAUDIE. Moment of madness, he was / trying to –

EILISH. Am I talkin' to you, Paudie?

KILIAN. Maybe I have.

EILISH. What?

KILIAN. Gone mad.

EILISH. Why d'you do it?

KILIAN. Just… this moment of madness.

EILISH. Stop talkin' shit an' tell me why / you did it?

KILIAN. Maybe Seamus an' me are just a little bit / mad.

EILISH. *Was!* Maybe he *was*! Now tell me why you did it or I swear to God, I'll ring the Guards myself!

Pause.

KILIAN. It was for Paudie's visa.

EILISH *looks at* PAUDIE.

PAUDIE. Don't look at me, he did this all on his own!

EILISH. This is Jimmy we're… he's an old man.

PAUDIE. This isn't who he is. This isn't who he is / at all –

EILISH. Oh shut up, Paudie! Just… shut up!

Silence. It's still raining outside.

PAUDIE (*gently*). Listen. It's dark out there, right? An' it's cold. An' it's pissing it down. Just makes everything feel worse than it really is.

KILIAN *and* EILISH *are looking at each other.*

Things'll be different in the morning. (*Pause.*) Hey. Eilish. His visa's come through. Great news, hah? It's come through.

EILISH *and* KILIAN *are still looking at each other.*

KILIAN. I can't.

PAUDIE. What d'you mean you can't?

KILIAN. I'm really sorry.

PAUDIE. What?

EILISH. No you're not.

Long pause.

But I can't help you with that.

EILISH *walks towards the door.*

PAUDIE. Ah don't go, Eilish.

EILISH (*turning back*). D'you know what, I'm sick've it.
Sick've the lot've ye. Sick've this place. And you? (*Pointing at* KILIAN.) You are fucked if you keep looking back! 'Cause nobody's coming to pick you up off that floor. If you lie down then that's where you'll stay 'cause we'll all be gone soon. Christ, Kilian, we'll all be gone. So where does that leave you? (*Pause.*) I was going to buy you a tie. For your first day on the job. I was going to buy you a new tie. Wasn't sure about the colour though. What colour would you've liked.

KILIAN. What?

EILISH. I said, what colour would you've liked?

KILIAN. What does it matter what colour / I would've liked?

EILISH. Just tell me what colour you would've / liked.

KILIAN. It doesn't fuckin' matter now though / does it?

EILISH. Tell me what you would've / liked!

KILIAN. Black, alright? Fuckin' black. Okay?

Pause.

EILISH. Yeah. Not what I had in mind. (*Looks at them both in turn.*) Good luck, lads. (*Exits.*)

The rain outside increases in ferocity. Like it's coming down in rivers. PAUDIE *pours a drink.*

PAUDIE. An' then there were two.

He toasts. He throws it back quickly.

6 a.m. the following morning. Day of the anniversary. Birdsong outside. PAUDIE *and* KILIAN *have stayed up all night. They're both knackered and have drunk themselves sober.* PAUDIE *is slumped at the bar, his head propped up in his hands. He's humming 'The Parting Glass', making strange sounds – opening his mouth wide, narrowing it, opening it again. Away in his own world sort of thing.*

PAUDIE. Can you remember the words to that? I used know all the words.

He yawns. Then he starts to hum again. KILIAN *is also sprawled on the bar, head resting on his arms, eyes closed.*

KILIAN. Paudie?

PAUDIE. Hmm?

KILIAN. Shut up. You sound like a dying hedgehog.

PAUDIE. Least I don't fuckin' look like one. (*Pause.*) Ah. Sure I was never the singer. We all know who the singer was. (*Gets up and walks to the window. Pulls the curtain back and looks outside. A small corridor of light spills into the room.*) Looks like spring might be here. 'Bout fuckin' time. (*Lets the curtain fall back. The room dims again. Turns and stretches, rubs his face hard.*) Kilian? Kil?

KILIAN *groans a response.*

I'm starving. Any crisps?

KILIAN *drags himself away from the bar and rummages for crisps. Throws a packet across to* PAUDIE, *then opens one for himself. They eat in silence.*

You should ring.

KILIAN. Ring who?

PAUDIE. The hospital.

KILIAN. S'too early.

PAUDIE. I mean later.

KILIAN. Course I will.

PAUDIE. Bet he's a lot better today.

They eat.

You should ring Eilish too. Just talk to her. It'll all work out in the end. Everything always works out in the end.

KILIAN *can't finish his crisps.*

Don't. Don't start. We've talked this out. I'm done.

KILIAN *starts eating again.* PAUDIE *eats too.*

Like I said, just give it back. No one needs to know. Fuck it, I'll do it. I'll go there an' I'll push it under his door myself an' that'll be an end to it.

KILIAN. Just like that?

PAUDIE. Just like that.

KILIAN. No. No, it's not your mess.

PAUDIE. Well then you do it! Through the letterbox. Under a flowerpot. Whatever. But just… do it!

Pause.

KILIAN. Yeah.

PAUDIE. Yeah?

KILIAN. Yeah.

PAUDIE. Praise the fuckin' Lord. (*Eats some more crisps.*) Now. We need to make a move. Big day today.

KILIAN. What?

PAUDIE. Big day today.

KILIAN *looks blank.*

Today? Nineteenth of April? Today's the nineteenth of April?

KILIAN *starts laughing.*

What's so funny?

KILIAN. I forgot.

PAUDIE. S'cause you're pissed.

KILIAN. I forgot today's the day.

PAUDIE *just looks at him. The laughter dies out.*

PAUDIE. Sober the fuck up, man.

Silence. PAUDIE *finishes his crisps.*

KILIAN. D'you ever wonder, Paudie? D'you ever wonder... what it's all about?

PAUDIE. Oh Jesus, you really are drunk.

KILIAN. I wonder all the time. Is that normal?

PAUDIE. Everyone fuckin' 'wonders'. We're all goin' round the place 'wondering'. But you have to know when to draw the line, else you'll wonder yerself into fuckin' oblivion.

KILIAN. I can feel him.

PAUDIE. What?

KILIAN. In here. Right now. I can. Sometimes I think I'm...

Silence.

PAUDIE. Started havin' this nightmare inside. Searching for him in the dark. We're in this field right? With torches. An' it's raining. Not heavy. Just drizzly, but no let-up y'know? Dirty old night. So I'm walkin' round callin' out for him an' next thing there's this sound. Like metal crunching. So I move towards it. The noise. Light bouncing off the torch, lightin' up bits of the hedges an' trees an' stuff. And then... I see him. 'Cause he's standing right in front of me. With his eyes closed. Fuckin' standing there, right in front of me, all pale an' washed-out with his eyes closed. So of course, I drop it. The torch. Stupid thing falls in the mud. I pick it up an' point it back at the same spot but... it's just black. Even the trees are gone.

Footsteps move around upstairs. They listen as they die away.

Sorry. I fuckin' hate it when people do that. Tell me their dreams. (*Long pause.*) D'you know what I think? I think something started to take over. An' it felt good when it happened. Something started takin' control, an' he wanted it to. But just for that second. So he went with it. Road's whipping by. Heart's pumping. But it's okay. It's all okay 'cause it's only meant to be fer a second. He just... went with it too long.

PAUDIE *walks to the window and pulls back the curtain again. Light spills into the room.*

Gonna be a beautiful day. Everything's always better in the morning. When the light's back. Too much rain here. Too much rain an' too much fog an' that's why Irish people are all depressed to fuck. It's like living in a giant quagmire.

He moves away from the window. The curtain falls back and the room dims again. PAUDIE *meanders around for a bit trying to sober up.* KILIAN *is deep in thought.* PAUDIE *notices a framed photo on the wall.*

Great day that.

KILIAN. Which one?

PAUDIE. Under-sixteen Hurling County Final, 2004.

KILIAN. Brilliant day.

PAUDIE. One goal. Five points.

KILIAN. Six.

PAUDIE. Six! Shit! You're right! Six points. Jesus, he was some little player, hah? Sun was out that day. You won the Munster Minor Final the week after. Everyone remembers that. You were like a fuckin' god after that. They started calling you Cúchulainn, for Christ's sake. Myra Collins was throwin' her knickers at ya. D'you remember her? Gorgeous she was. In London now. (*Pause.*) Maybe I should go.

KILIAN. London?

PAUDIE. Dublin.

KILIAN. To be a security guard at Lidls?

PAUDIE. I hear the cheese section is a constant target. Sure it'll help me get into shape. I'm startin' to fill out y'know.

(*Looking at picture again.*) The glory years, hah? Got my car loan that year. Fuckin' eighteen years old an' self-employed but not a bother.

KILIAN. Expensive loan.

PAUDIE. Lovely car though. (*Pause.*) What time are people coming?

KILIAN (*pouring another drink*). Noon. D'you want one?

PAUDIE. Nah. I should head. Shower. Eat. Sleep a bit. Can't drink our lives away I s'pose. (*Looks at* KILIAN.) You have to go, man. You have to. They fuckin' love the Irish out there.

KILIAN. They don't y'know.

PAUDIE. Hah?

KILIAN. Like us that much. They don't. In fact, I'd go so far as to say they don't fuckin' like us at all, 'cause all we do out there is get pissed an' throw punches an' clog up their A&E wards 'cause we can't be arsed with the sunscreen.

Pause.

PAUDIE. You've got a really low opinion of yourself. That's your problem. I need a piss. (*Goes to exit.*)

KILIAN. Think you won't have nightmares in Australia?

PAUDIE *turns back.*

That you won't be searching in the dark out there?

PAUDIE. Go make some coffee.

KILIAN. That you won't still wonder 'bout what you could've done?

PAUDIE. Would you shut up talkin' like that / would ya?

KILIAN. That those thoughts won't be spinning round inside / your head?

PAUDIE. Shut the fuck up, Kilian!

Pause. PAUDIE *exits to toilets.* KILIAN *remains where he is, thinking. After a bit, toilet flushes and* PAUDIE *re-enters. He looks at his friend for a moment.*

D'you remember when Tom Moriarty's baby cousin died of a cot death? You were nine years old. Nine years old an' you thought it was your fault. D'you remember? Convinced you'd thought something, or said something, or taken a feckin' piss the wrong way and that baby died 'cause of it. Jesus Christ, man. Enough. For once in your life, draw the fuckin' line and give yourself a break. (*Pause.*) Alright. Say we made a mistake. Right? We missed something. Okay? We fucked up. Christ, holding my hands up here like. Padraig O'Sullivan has fucked up many a time but d'you know what? I'm still no write-off. An' neither are you. 'Cause nothing's ever that clear-cut. We make choices but there are reasons an' I won't write myself off, man. I won't. 'Cause what chance would I have then? (*Pause.*) Now. I'm gonna go. Need to sort myself out but I'll be back for twelve. Want me to open the curtains?

KILIAN *shakes his head.*

Then go upstairs an' get some sleep.

KILIAN. A good laugh an' a long sleep, hah?

PAUDIE. The two best cures.

They go to the door. KILIAN *unlocks it for him.*

It'll all work out in the end.

KILIAN *nods his head.* PAUDIE *exits.*

KILIAN. Hey, Paudie?

PAUDIE *reappears at the doorway.*

PAUDIE. Wha'?

Long pause.

KILIAN. Nothin'.

PAUDIE. Thought you had a joke fer me there.

KILIAN. Forgot it.

PAUDIE. Hate when that happens. Might come back to you in a bit.

KILIAN. Yeah.

PAUDIE. Right. I'm off. I'll see ya soon.

KILIAN. See ya.

PAUDIE leaves. KILIAN locks the door after him. He goes back to the bar and starts clearing up a bit, but can't muster the energy to finish. A strange sort of quietness descends. He walks over to the same picture PAUDIE had been looking at. He stares at it for a while.

Then he moves to the window and in one swift movement, he pulls the curtains back. Light floods into the room. It's piercingly bright and hurts his eyes. He stands there for a long time looking out.

He walks behind the bar and goes out the back for a moment. When he returns, he's wearing his jacket and has a set of car keys in his hand.

He looks up at the ceiling.

He looks at the picture.

The light in the room starts to change.

We hear a loud burst of laughter from the smoking area just outside. Then a toilet flushes and JIMMY appears. He closes the curtains and the room dims again, then makes his way over to the bar and sits on a stool. KILIAN is still looking at the picture. EILISH then enters, finishing a conversation with someone outside –

EILISH. D'you know what, Seamus? I'd marry a sheep quicker than I'd marry you.

JIMMY. What's that?

EILISH. Seamus just asked me to marry him again.

JIMMY. Did he now? Was there a ring?

EILISH. One made out've beer labels.

PAUDIE enters from outside, calling behind him –

PAUDIE. I swear to God, man, you should be barred for talkin' shite! (*Grabs KILIAN by the shoulders as he speaks, jolting him from one world into another.*) Can we bar him, Kil? Please? Keeps sayin' it should've been passed up the field to the forwards instead of a midfielder takin' it.

EILISH (*outraged, calling to person outside*). He would've passed it to ya if you'd not been so busy preenin' yerself out on the pitch!

PAUDIE. Exactly! Don't mind him, man, that goal was beautiful.

EILISH. Right on the stroke of the whistle.

JIMMY. Cúchulainn here knows how to take the game by the scruff of the neck, hah?

PAUDIE. Ye fuckin' carved open that defence like!

JIMMY. Power an' pace, an' ya steered the side home.

PAUDIE (*calling out again*). Even with a useless forward who can't mark his man for shit!

Jeers from outside.

Ah go suck on a lemon! (*To the others.*) To Cúchulainn!

They salute and drink.

JIMMY. That reminds me of a story.

PAUDIE. Oh no, here we go.

EILISH. Shut up, Paudie.

PAUDIE. Sure half the time he tells the same fuckin' story over an' over again. Oh yeah, I can't wait for anoth– (*Throws his head back and snores. Quick as a flash,* EILISH *elbows him off the bar.*)

JIMMY (*to* PAUDIE). Who'll tell them after I'm gone, hah? Ye'll have to tell them yerselves then so ye will.

PAUDIE *rolls his eyes.*

KILIAN. Go on, Jim. We're listening.

JIMMY. It was 1963. Kilburn, London. Friday night an' the work was done. Hard ol' slog on the roads back then so it was. Anyway, a group've us were goin' down the dance hall that night. Clancy Brothers were in town see.

PAUDIE. Ah, the Clancy Brothers. Didn't they do great things altogether for the Aran / sweater.

EILISH. Shhhhh!

JIMMY. We used congregate in a pub on the High Road called
    The Green Robin. Good gang've us there'd be. Donach
    O'Mahony from Dingle, Jack Hannafin an' Kieran
    O'Sullivan from Castlemaine, Fergus Mulcahy from lovely
    Macroom. Oh built like a brick shithouse Fergus was – great
    to have round in a brawl. And who were the others now?

PAUDIE*'s taking the piss behind* JIMMY*'s back.* EILISH *is
    glaring at him.*

Oh that's right, Barry Egan from out the way in Lixnaw.
    Brendan Hegarty from two mile down the road. An' there
    was one more... Muiris Fitzgerald! Jesus, how could I forget
    Muiris. Great friend he was. Got the boat over together an'
    he's still there so he is. Buried in Lewisham graveyard.

PAUDIE. Christ Almighty! When're we gettin' to the good bit?!

KILIAN. I'll bar you in a minute if you don't shut up.

JIMMY. So. There we all were. Gathered together round our
    pints, gearing up for what would turn out to be one of the
    best nights of my life if I remember correctly. Oh there was
    dancing to be had that night let me tell you. The chat an' the
    craic was a-flowin' an' the place was fillin' up with all the
    lads an' lassies in fer a little drink afore heading down the
    road to the dance hall. An' Brendan Hegarty was just sayin'
    we should make a move to avoid the queues, when don't I
    catch sight of this big brute of a navvy elbowing his way out
    from the bar. Mad eyes like, with a big grizzly head on him
    an' a gigantic red cobra tattooed on his right arm. An' he
    pushin' an' shovin' his way through with his pint balancing
    precariously in one hand. An' then next thing, doesn't he slip
    an' lose his footing. An' the pint goes flying up into the air
    an' comes down all over Fergus's head, the glass smashing
    into smithereens as it hits the side of his rockhard skull.
    Well! There's a big hush then in the place. All the eyes on the
    two of 'em – the fella from Ireland as big as a boat an' the
    English navvy with the cobra tattoo. Everyone waiting to see
    which way they'll need to duck when the punches go flying,
    an' what does Fergus do? He just looks at yer man, then he
    looks down at himself all soaked in good beer, an' he says,
    'Sure it's something to suck on the way home!'

Everyone laughs except PAUDIE.

PAUDIE. Right. So basically, this one fella comes into a pub an' buys a pint, an' then he spills it on this other fella? Oh yeah, great fuckin' story there, Jim. D'you've the film rights to that like?

EILISH *and* KILIAN *try not to laugh but can't help it.* JIMMY *just glares at him.*

Cinemas'll be packed to the rafters fer that one. Johnny Depp'll be after the lead in it. An' Tom Cruise'd be great as the fella who spills the bit've his pint. (*Big burst of laughter.*) That was two minutes off my life that was.

JIMMY. Cheeky pup.

KILIAN. Ah, sure he's only messin' with ya.

EILISH. It was a great story, Jim.

We can hear something now. A solitary voice singing 'The Parting Glass' and the voice is beautiful.

PAUDIE. I mean, that's nearly as good as the one 'bout the fella who answered the phone an' then took down a message.

EILISH. Shhhh.

PAUDIE. Christ, Jim boy, s'bout as interesting as a fishing story like. Or one about golf. Or a story about someone's dream!

EILISH. Paudie, would ya shut up!

A hush descends and we can hear the voice clearly now, drifting in from outside.

EILISH *wanders over to the door and leans against it, arms folded, listening.* JIMMY *sits back in his chair and closes his eyes.* PAUDIE *sips at his pint and* KILIAN *leans over the bar with his head bowed.*

The singing continues.

The light fades.

End of play.

A Nick Hern Book

Coolatully first published in Great Britain in 2014 as a paperback original by Nick Hern Books Limited, The Glasshouse, 49a Goldhawk Road, London W12 8QP, in association with Papatango and the Finborough Theatre

Coolatully copyright © 2014 Fiona Doyle

Fiona Doyle has asserted her moral right to be identified as the author of this work

Cover image: Mark Waldron

Designed and typeset by Nick Hern Books, London
Printed in the UK by Mimeo Ltd, Huntingdon, Cambridgeshire PE29 6XX

A CIP catalogue record for this book is available from the British Library

ISBN 978 1 84842 434 0

CAUTION All rights whatsoever in this play are strictly reserved. Requests to reproduce the text in whole or in part should be addressed to the publisher.

Amateur Performing Rights Applications for performance, including readings and excerpts, by amateurs in the English language throughout the world should be addressed to the Performing Rights Manager, Nick Hern Books, The Glasshouse, 49a Goldhawk Road, London W12 8QP, *tel* +44 (0)20 8749 4953, *e-mail* info@nickhernbooks.co.uk, except as follows:

Australia: Dominie Drama, 8 Cross Street, Brookvale 2100, *tel* (2) 9938 8686, *fax* (2) 9938 8695, *e-mail* drama@dominie.com.au

New Zealand: Play Bureau, PO Box 9013, St Clair, Dunedin 9047, *tel* (3) 455 9959, *e-mail* play.bureau.nz@xtra.co.nz

South Africa: DALRO (pty) Ltd, PO Box 31627, 2017 Braamfontein, *tel* (11) 712 8000, *fax* (11) 403 9094, *e-mail* theatricals@dalro.co.za

United States of America and Canada: Curtis Brown Ltd, see details below.

Professional Performing Rights Application for performance by professionals in any medium and in any language throughout the world should be addressed to Curtis Brown Ltd, Haymarket House, 28–29 Haymarket, London SW1Y 4SP, *tel* +44 (0)20 7393 4400, *fax* +44 (0)20 7393 4401, *e-mail* cb@curtisbrown.co.uk

No performance of any kind may be given unless a licence has been obtained. Applications should be made before rehearsals begin. Publication of this play does not necessarily indicate its availability for amateur performance.

www.nickhernbooks.co.uk

facebook.com/nickhernbooks

twitter.com/nickhernbooks